CAVOUR

CAVOUR

BY

THE COUNTESS
EVELYN MARTINENGO CESARESCO

Italia ab exteris liberanda.
Motto of Pope JULIUS II.

MACMILLAN AND CO., LIMITED
ST. MARTIN'S STREET, LONDON

1924

PREFACE

" Je suis italien avant tout, et c'est pour faire jouir à mon pays
du *self government* à l'intérieur, comme à l'extérieur, que j'ai
entrepris la rude tâche de chasser l'Autriche de l'Italie sans y
substituer la domination d'aucune autre Puissance."—*Cavour to
the Marquis Emmanuel d'Azeglio (May* 8, 1860).

THE day is passed when the warmest admirer of the
eminent man whose character is sketched in the following pages would think it needful to affirm that he alone
regenerated his country.   Many forces were at work :
the energising impulse of moral enthusiasm, the spell of
heroism, the ancient and still unextinguished potency of
kingly headship.   But Cavour's hand controlled the
working of these forces, and compelled them to coalesce.

The first point in his plan was to make Piedmont a
lever by which Italy could be raised.   An Englishman,
Lord William Bentinck, conceived an identical plan in
which Sicily stood for Piedmont.   He failed ; Cavour
succeeded.   The second point was to cause the Austrian
power in Italy to receive such a shock that, whether it
succumbed at once or not, it would never recover.   In
this too, with the help of Napoleon III., he succeeded.
The third point was to prevent the Continental Powers
from forcibly impeding Italian Unity when it became
plain that the population desired to be united.   This
Cavour succeeded in doing with the help of England.

Time, which beautifies unlovely things, begins to cast its glamour over the old Italian *régimes*. It is forgotten how low the Italian race had fallen under puny autocrats whose influence was soporific when not vicious. The vigorous if turbulent life of the Middle Ages was extinct; proof abounded that the *rôle* of small states was played out. Goldsmith's description, severe as it is, was not unmerited—

> Here may be seen, in bloodless pomp array'd,
> The pasteboard triumph and the cavalcade;
> Processions formed for piety and love,
> A mistress or a saint in every grove.
> By sports like these are all their cares beguil'd,
> The sports of children satisfy the child;
> Each nobler aim, represt by long control,
> Now sinks at last, or feebly mans the soul.

Only those who do not know the past can turn away from the present with scorn or despair. In this century a nation has arisen which, in spite of all its troubles, is alive with ambition, industry, movement; which has ten thousand miles of railway, which has conquered the malaria at Rome, which has doubled its population and halved its death-rate, which sends out great battle-ships from Venice and Spezia, Castellamare and Taranto. This nation is Cavour's memorial : *si monumentum requiris circumspice.*

SALÒ, LAGO DI GARDA.

CONTENTS

CHAPTER I

CHAPTER VII

CHAPTER VIII

CHAPTER IX

CHAPTER X

CHAPTER XI

CHAPTER XII

CHAPTER XIII

CHAPTER I

HEREDITY AND ENVIRONMENT

NOTHING is permanent but change; only it ought to be remembered that change itself is of the nature of an evolution, not of a catastrophe. Commonly this is not remembered, and we seem to go forward by bounds and leaps, or it may be to go backward; in either case the thread of continuity is lost. We appear to have moved far away from the men of forty years ago, except in the instances in which these men have survived to remind us of themselves. It is rather startling to recollect that Cavour might have been among the survivors. He was born on August 10, 1810. The present Pope, Leo the Thirteenth, was born in the same year.

It was a moment of lull, after the erection and before the collapse of the Napoleonic edifice in Italy. If no thinking mind believed that edifice to be eternal, if every day did not add to its solidity but took something silently from it, nevertheless it had the outwardly imposing appearance which obtains for a political *régime* the acceptance of the apathetic and lukewarm to supplement the support of partisans. Above all, it was a

S   B

phase in national existence which made any real return to the phase that preceded it impossible. The air teemed with new germs; they entered even into the mysterious composition of the brain of the generation born in the first decade of the nineteenth century.

Environment and heredity do not explain all the puzzle of any single man's mind and character, but they form co-efficients in the making of him which can be no longer disregarded. The chief point to be noticed in reference to Cavour is that he was the outcome of a mingling of race which was not only transmitted through the blood, but also was a living presence during his childhood and youth. His father's stock, the Bensos of Cavour, belonged to the old Piedmontese nobility. A legend declares that a Saxon pilgrim, a follower of Frederick Barbarossa, stopped, when returning from the Holy Land, in the little republic of Chieri, where he met and married the heiress to all the Bensos, whose name he assumed. Cavour used to laugh at the story, but the cockle shells in the arms of the Bensos and their German motto, "Gott will recht," seem to connect the family with those transalpine crusading adventurers who brought the rising sap of a new nation to reinvigorate the peoples they tarried amongst. Chieri formed a diminutive free community known as "the republic of the seven B's," from the houses of Benso, Balbo, Balbiani, Biscaretti, Buschetti, Bertone, and Broglie, which took their origin from it, six of which became notable in their own country and one in France. The Bensos acquired possession of the fief of Santena and of the old fastness of Cavour in the province of Pignerolo. This castle has remained a ruin since it was destroyed by Catinat, but in the last century Charles Emmanuel III. conferred the title of Marquis of Cavour on a Benso who had rendered distinguished military services. At the time of Cavour's birth the palace of the Bensos at Turin contained a complete and varied society composed of all sorts of nationalities and temperaments. Such different elements could hardly have dwelt together in harmony if the head of the household, Cavour's grandmother, had not been a superior woman in every sense, and one endowed with the worldly tact and elastic spirits without which even superior gifts are of little worth in the delicate, intimate relations of life. Nurtured in a romantic *château* on the lake of Annecy, Philippine, daughter of the Marquis de Sales, was affianced by her father at an early age to the eldest son of the Marquis Benso di Cavour, knight of the Annunziata, whom she never saw till the day of their marriage. At once she took her place in her new family not only as the ideal *grande dame*, but as the person to whom every one went in trouble and perplexity. That was a moment which developed strong characters and effaced weak ones. The revolutionary ocean was fatally rolling towards the Alps. It found what had been so long the "buffer state" asleep. There was a king who, unlike the princes of his race, was more amiable than vigorous. Arthur Young, the traveller, reports that Victor Emmanuel I. went about with his pocket full of bank notes, and was discontented at night if he had not given them all away. "Yet this," adds the observant Englishman, "with an empty treasury and an incomplete, ill-paid army." It was a bad preparation for the deluge, but when that arrived, inevitable though unforeseen, desperate if futile efforts were made to stem it. Some of the Piedmontese nobility were very rich, but it was a wealth of increment, not of capital. The burdens imposed when too late by the Sardinian Government, and afterwards the cost of the French occupation, severely strained the resources even of the wealthiest. The Marquise Philippine sold the family plate and the splendid hangings of silk brocade which adorned the walls of the Palazzo Cavour at Turin. Napoleon from the first looked upon Italy as the bank of the French army. This idea had been impressed upon him before he started for the campaign which was to prove the corner-stone of his career. "He was instructed," writes the secret agent Landrieux, "as to what might well be drawn from this war for the French treasury."

After the pillage and the war contributions came the blood-tax. The Marquise Philippine's son, sixteen years old, was ordered to join General Berthier's corps, and to provide him with £10 pocket money she sold what till then she had religiously kept, a silver holy water stoup, which belonged to her saintly ancestor, François de Sales.

The last sacrifices, imposed not in the name of the country, but to the advantage of an insatiable invader, were not likely to inspire the old nobility of Piedmont with much love for the new order of things, nor was love the feeling with which the Marquise regarded it, but she had the insight to see what few of her class perceived, that the hour of day cannot be turned back; the future could not be as the past had been. When Prince Camillo Borghese was appointed governor of Piedmont (on account of his being the husband of Napoleon's sister, the beautiful Pauline Bonaparte, who was the original of Canova's Venus), the Marquise

Philippine was commanded to accept the post of *dame d'honneur* to the Princess. A refusal would have meant the ruin of both the Cavours and her own kin, the De Sales, whose estates in Savoy were already confiscated. She bowed to necessity, and in a position which could not have been one of the easiest, she knew how to preserve her own dignity, and to win the friendship of the far from demure Pauline, whom she accompanied to Paris for the celebration of the marriage of Napoleon with Marie Louise. It is characteristic of the epoch that in the French capital the Marquise took lessons in the art of teaching from a French pedagogue then in repute, to qualify her to begin the education of her little grandchildren, Gustave and Camille.

These two boys were the sons of the Marquis Michele Benso, who had married a daughter of the Count de Sellon of Geneva. While on a tour in Switzerland to recover his health from a wound received in the French service, the Marquis met the Count and his three daughters, of whom he wished to make the eldest, Victoire, his wife ; but on his suit not prospering with her, he proposed to and was accepted by the second daughter, Adèle. After an unfortunate first marriage, Victoire became the Duchess de Clermont Tonnerre, and the youngest sister, Henriette, married a Count d'Auzers of Auvergne. All these relatives ended by taking up their abode in the Palazzo Cavour at Turin. Victoire was the cleverest, but her sisters as well as herself were what even in these days would be considered highly educated. She became a Roman Catholic, a step followed by Adèle after the birth of her second child, Camille, but Henriette remained true to the rigid Protestantism

of Geneva. At the christening of Camille de Cavour
the Prince and Princess Borghese officiated as sponsors,
the Marquis Benso holding at that time a post in the
Prince's household which he owed to the good graces
enjoyed by his mother.

It is plain that of all his kindred, the charming and
valiant Marquise Philippine was the one whom Camille
de Cavour most fondly loved. She was the member of
his family who understood him best not only in childhood, but in manhood, and when all the others reproached
him with embracing ideas contrary to his traditions and
his order, he turned for comfort to his "dearest
Marina," as he called her ("Marina" being the pet-
name by which children in Piedmont called their grand-
mothers), and begged her to defend him against the
charge of undutiful conduct. It might be true, he said,
with the irony which was one day to become so familiar,
that he was that dreadful thing, a liberal, but devoid of
natural feeling he was not. On the great day when the
Statute was granted, he said to the light-hearted old
lady, "Marina, we get on capitally, you and I; you
were always a little bit of a Jacobin." That was not
long before her strength, though not her courage, gave
way under the deep sorrow of the loss of her great-
grandson Auguste on the field of Goito. She died in
the midst of the political transformation she had so long
waited for.

As a child Cavour was normally sweet-tempered, but
subject to violent fits of passion; while he hated his
lessons, he showed an early development of intelligence
and judgment. Like most precocious children he had
one or two infantile love affairs. A letter exists written

when he was six, in which he upbraids a little girl
named Fanchonette for basely abandoning him.   He
says that he loves her still, *but* he has now made the
acquaintance of a young lady of extraordinary charms,
who has twice taken him out in the most beautiful gilt
carriage.   It is amusing to note the worldly wisdom of
the suitor of six who reckons on jealousy to bring back
the allegiance of the fair but faithless Fanchonette.
The magnificent rival was Silvio Pellico's friend, the
Marchioness de Barolo, who, like every one else, was
attracted by the clever child with his blue eyes and
little round face.   Another story belonging to the same
date is even more characteristic.   The Cavours went
every year to Switzerland to stay with their connections,
the De Sellons and the De la Rives.   On this occasion,
when the travellers reached M. de la Rive's villa at
Présinge, Camille, looking terribly in earnest, and with
an air of importance, made the more comical by the
little red costume he was wearing, went straight to his
host with the announcement that the postmaster had
treated them abominably by giving them the worst
horses, and that he ought to be dismissed.   "But," said
M. de la Rive, "I cannot dismiss him ; that depends on
the syndic."   "Very well," said the child, "I wish for
an audience with the syndic."   "You shall have one
to-morrow," replied M. de la Rive, who wrote to the
syndic, a friend of his, that he was going to send him
a highly entertaining little man.   Camille was therefore
received next day with all possible ceremony, which by
no means abashed him.   After making three bows, he
quietly and lucidly explained his grievance, and apparently got a promise of satisfaction, as when he went

back he exclaimed in triumph to M. de la Rive, "He will be dismissed!"

The Swiss relations were most enlightened people. Cavour's uncle, the Count de Sellon, was a sort of Swiss Wilberforce, an ardent philanthropist whose faith in human perfectibility used sometimes to make his nephew smile, but early intercourse with a man of such large and generous views could not have been without effect. De Sellon was one of the first persons to dream of arbitration, and though a Protestant he sent a memorial on this subject to the Pope. M. de la Rive was a man of great scientific acquirements, and his son William became Cavour's congenial and life-long friend. This cosmopolitan society was entirely unlike the narrow coteries of the ancient Piedmontese aristocracy which are so graphically described by Massimo d'Azeglio, and the absence of constraint in which Cavour grew up makes a striking contrast to the iron paternal rule under which the young d'Azeglios trembled. It should be observed, however, that in spite of his mixed blood and scattered ties, Cavour was in feeling from the first the member of one race and the citizen of one state. The stronger influence, that of the father's strain, predominated to the exclusion of all others. Though all classes in Piedmont till within the last fifty years spoke French when they did not speak dialect, the intellectual sway of France was probably nowhere in Italy felt so little as in Piedmont. The proximity of the two countries tended not for it, but against it. They had been often at war; all the memories of the Piedmontese people, the heroic exploit of Pietro Micca, the royal legend of the Superga, turned on resistance to the powerful neighbour. A long line of territorial nobles like the Bensos transmits, if nothing else, at least a strong sentiment for the birthland. In Cavour this sentiment was, indeed, to widen even in boyhood, but it widened into Italian patriotism, not into sterile cosmopolitanism.

In one respect Cavour was brought up according to the strictest of old Piedmontese conventions. No one forgot that he was a younger son. Gustave, the elder brother, received a classical education, and acquired a strong taste for metaphysics. He became a thinker rather than a man of action, and was one of the first and staunchest friends of the philosopher-theologian Rosmini, whose attempts to reconcile religion and philosophy led him into a bitter struggle with Rome. For Camille another sort of life was planned. It was decided that he must "do something," and at the age of ten he was sent to the Military Academy at Turin. He did not like it, but it was better for him than if he had been kept at home. Mathematics were well taught at the Academy, and in this branch he soon outstripped all his schoolfellows. He himself always spoke of his mathematical studies as having been of great service in forming the habit of precise thought ; from the study of triangles, he said, he went on to the study of men and things. On the other hand the boys were taught little Latin and less Greek, and nothing was done to furnish them with the basis of a literary style, a fact always deplored by Cavour, who insisted that the art of writing ought to be acquired when young ; otherwise it could not be practised without labour, and never with entire success. He once said that he found it easier to make

Italy than a sonnet. In his own case he regretted never having become a ready writer, because he knew that the pen is a force ; he held that a man should cultivate every means at his disposal to increase his power.

In 1824, when Charles Albert returned to Piedmont after three years' exile in consequence of the part he was suspected of having taken in the abortive revolution of 1821, one of his first acts was to obtain a nomination for young Cavour as page in the royal household. The pages were all inmates of the Military Academy, where the expense of their education was borne by the king after they received the appointment. The Count d'Auzers, a strong Legitimist, was one of the oldest friends of the Prince of Carignano, who was regarded at the Palazzo Cavour as the victim of false accusations of liberalism. Charles Albert always seemed to reflect the opinions of the person to whom he was writing or speaking. Thus it is certain that in his letters to the Count he appeared as a convinced upholder of white flags. Cavour must have heard him often defended from the charge of patriotism. Perhaps this created in his mind a first aversion, which was strengthened by personal contact in the course of his duties at Court. At any rate it is clear that he never liked or trusted him.

When Cavour left the Military Academy in 1826 he came out first in the final examinations. He entered the army with the rank of lieutenant in the Corps of Engineers. He began to learn English. In a letter written at this time he speaks of the utility of modern languages and a real knowledge of history, but adds that a man who wishes to make a name should concentrate his faculties rather than disperse them among too many subjects and pursuits. Even then he had an almost definite project of preparing himself to play a part in life. There is not much to show what were his political ideas, except a memorandum written when he was eighteen on the Piedmontese revolution of 1821, in which he adopted the views of Santorre di Santa Rosa, once Charles Albert's friend and later his severest critic, to combat whose indictment the Count d'Auzers had written folios in the French and German newspapers. At the end of the memorandum Cavour transcribed an extract from Santa Rosa's work, in which he invoked the advent of an Italian Washington. Was that the part which Cavour dreamed of playing? A few years after, he wrote in a fit of despondency, " There was a time when I should have thought it the most natural thing in the world that I should wake up one morning prime minister of a kingdom of Italy." The words written in 1832 throw a flood of light on the subjects of his boyish dreams and the goal of his prophetic ambition.

The story repeated by most of Cavour's biographers, that in putting off the page's uniform he uttered some scornful words which, reported to Charles Albert, changed the goodwill of that prince into hostility, rests on doubtful authority; but it seems to be true that Charles Albert, who began by being very well disposed to the son and nephew of his friends, calling him in one letter " the interesting youth who justifies such great hopes," and in another, " ce charmant Camille," came to consider his quondam *protégé* a restless spirit, inconvenient in the present and possibly dangerous in the

future.   Though the schoolboy essay above mentioned
was kept a secret, the liberal heresies of the young
lieutenant were well enough known.   He was told that
he would bring father and mother in sorrow to the
grave, and he was even threatened with banishment to
America.   The police watched his movements.   He
wrote to his Swiss uncle that he had no right to com-
plain as he was liberal and very liberal and desired a
complete change in the whole system.   On Charles
Albert's accession to the throne he was sent to the
solitary Alpine fortress of Bard ; but it appears that not
the king (as he supposed) but his own father suggested
the step.   Cavour saw in the idleness and apathy of
garrison life in this lonely place a type of the disease
from which the whole State was suffering.   He wrote
to the Count de Sellon, the apostle of universal peace,
that much as he abhorred bloodshed, he could think of
no cure but war.   " The Italians need regeneration ;
their *moral*, which was completely corrupted under the
ignoble dominion of Spaniards and Austrians, regained a
little energy under the French *régime*, and the ardent
youth of the country sighs for a nationality ; but to
break entirely with the past, to be born anew to a better
state, great efforts are necessary and sacrifices of all
kinds must remould the Italian character.   An Italian
war would be a sure pledge that we were going to
become again a nation, that we were rising from the
mud in which we have been trampled for so many
centuries."

These lines, written by a young officer of twenty-one,
show how far Cavour had already outstripped the
Piedmontese provincialism which had the upper hand

in the early years of Charles Albert's reign. He described himself as vegetating, but he was not idle; sustained mental activity was, in fact, a necessity to him whatever were his outward circumstances. He read Bentham and Adam Smith, and was excited by the events going on in England, then in the throes of the first Reform Bill. It was in the fortress of Bard that he gained a grasp of English politics which he never lost, and which hardly another foreigner ever possessed in a like degree. By chance he became acquainted with an English artist who was engaged in making drawings of the Alpine passes. This gave him not only the opportunity of speaking and writing English, but also of expressing his private thoughts without reserve, which was impossible with his fellow-countrymen. Throughout his life he found the same mental relaxation in his intercourse with Englishmen; he felt safe with them.

Cavour was not meant to be a soldier; his tastes did not agree with the routine of military life, and his clear judgment told him that the army is not the natural or correct sphere for a politician—which he knew himself to be even then, in a country where politics may be said not to have existed. Acting on these reflections, he resigned his commission, and his father, perhaps to keep him quiet, bought him a small independent property near the ancestral estate at Leri. The Marquis warned his son that the income would not allow him to keep a valet or a horse; his mother opposed the purchase, as she thought that the young landlord would be tempted to spend more than he had, but to this his father replied that if a man was not a man at twenty-five he would be

one never. The Marquis Michele Benso had recently
assumed the post of *Vicario* of Turin, which his family
thought below his dignity, but he apparently took it to
oblige the king, with whom the *Vicario*, who was a sort
of Prefect of Police, was in daily contact. As a result,
the estate of Leri, which had been neglected before, was
now going actually to ruin. Cavour, with the approval
of his brother, proposed to undertake the whole management of the property, an offer gladly accepted, as the
Marquis was well convinced that his younger son had
rather too many than too few abilities. Cavour saw in
agriculture the only field at present open to him. When
he left the army he scarcely knew a cabbage from a
turnip, for he had not been brought up in the country,
but in a few years he familiarised himself with everything connected with the subject, from the most homely
detail to wide scientific generalisations. With knowledge
came interest, which, absent at first, grew strong, and
lasted all his life. Little, he said, does the outsider
know the charm of planting a field of potatoes or rearing
a young heifer ! The practical experience which Cavour
gained was precious. How many cabinet ministers in
different parts of the world would lead to bankruptcy a
farm, a factory, a warehouse, even a penny tart shop !
As a matter of fact, one Italian minister of finance was
legally interdicted, on the application of his family, from
managing his own estates.

Leri, which Cavour looked upon henceforth as his
true home, lies in one of the ugliest parts of the plains
of Piedmont, cold in winter, scorched by a burning sun
in summer, and unhealthy from the exhalations of the
rice-fields which contribute to its wealth. Except that

game was tolerably plentiful, it had none of the attractions of an English country-seat—the smiling hillside,
the ancestral elms, the park, the garden. Cavour led
the simplest life; the old housekeeper who cooked the
dinner also placed it on the table. But the fare, if
plain, was abundant, and Cavour was delighted to
entertain his friends and neighbours, who found him the
most affable of hosts, inexhaustibly good-tempered, a
patient listener, a talker abounding in wit and wisdom.
He had the art of adapting himself perfectly to the
society in which he moved, but in one thing he was
always the same: wherever he went he carried his
intense vitality—that quality of *entrain* which persuades
more than eloquence or earnestness. He induced others
to join him in experiments which were then innovations:
steam-mills, factories for artificial manures and the like,
while the machinery and new methods introduced at
Leri revolutionised farming in Piedmont. One great
scheme planned by him, an irrigatory canal between the
Ticino and the Po, was only finished after his death, as
the most worthy tribute to his memory. He rose at
four, went to see his cattle, stood in the broiling harvest
fields to overlook the reapers, acted, in short, as his own
bailiff, and to these habits he returned in later years,
whenever he had time to visit Leri. Cavour's mind was
not poetic; we hear of his admiring only one poet,
Shakespeare, but in Shakespeare it was probably the
deep knowledge of man that attracted him, the apprehension of how men with given passions must act under
given conditions. He did not, therefore, see country
pursuits from a poet's standpoint, but he appreciated
their power of calming men's minds, of dissipating the

fog of unrealities, of tending towards what Kant called,
in a phrase he quoted with approval, " practical reason."
He considered, also, that nothing can so assure the
stability of a nation as an intelligent interest shared by
a large portion of its citizens in the cultivation of the
soil.   The English country gentleman who divided his
time between his duties in Parliament and those not
less obligatory on his estates was in Cavour's eyes an
almost ideal personage.   It should be added that Cavour
could not understand a country life which did not
embrace solicitude for the worker. The true agriculturist
gained the confidence of the poor around him ; it was,
he said, so easy to gain it.   He was kindly, thoughtful,
and just in his treatment of his dependents, and he
always retained his hold on their affections ; when Italy
was asking what she should do without her great statesman, the sorrowing peasants of Leri asked in tears what
they should do without their master ?

One passage in Cavour's early life was revealed a few
years ago, and, whether or not it was right to reveal it,
the portrait would be now incomplete which did not
touch upon it.   The episode belongs to the critical
psychological moment in his development : the time
immediately after he left the army, and before he found
an outlet for his activity, and, what was more essential
to him, a purpose and an object not in the distance but
straight before him, in the care of his father's acres.
His position at home was not happy ; his brother's small
children were of more importance in the household than
himself, and when Cavour once administered a well-
merited correction to the much-spoilt eldest born, the
Marquis Gustave threw a chair at his head.   Between

the brothers in after life there prevailed remarkable and
unbroken harmony, but it is easy to see that when first
grown to manhood Gustave presumed rather selfishly on
his *rôle* of heir, while Camille took too seriously the
supposed discovery that he was "necessary to no one!"
Beyond all this, there was the undeclared clash of the
new with the old, the feeling of having moved apart,
which produces a moral vacuum until, by and by, it is
realised that the value of the first affections and ties
depends precisely on their resting on no basis of opinion.
Cavour was overwhelmed by a sense of isolation; if he
decided "like Hamlet" (so he writes in his diary) to
abstain from suicide, he believed that he wished himself
heartily out of the world.   To his family he seemed an
abnormal and unnatural young man.   A conversation is
on record which took place between the two childless
aunts who lived with the Cavours.   The date was just
before Cavour's departure on a first visit to Paris.
"Did you remark," said Mme. Victoire, "how indifferent
Camille seemed when I spoke to him of the Paris
theatres?   I really do not know what will interest him
on his travels; the poor boy is entirely absorbed in
revolutions."   "It is quite true," replied Mme. Henriette;
"Camille has no curiosity about things, he cares for
nothing but politics."   And the two ladies went on to
draw melancholy prognostics from their nephew's study
of political economy, "an erroneous and absolutely
useless science."

A charming countess who had made a favourite of
Cavour in his boyhood tried to extract a promise from
him that he would never again mix himself up in
politics; he refused to give it; sooner or later, he writes

C

in his diary, she would have blushed for him had he
consented.   But, he adds bitterly, what was the good of
demanding such a promise from one for whom politically
everything was ended ?   " Ah ! if I were an Englishman,
by this time I should be something and my name would
not be wholly unknown ! "   Here, again, was a source
of depression.   At the Military Academy he had formed
one almost romantic comradeship with a delicate and
reserved youth, some years older than himself, Baron
Severino Cassio, to whom he first confided his determination to Italianise himself : to study the language, history,
laws, customs of the whole country with a view to preparing for the future.   Cassio presciently marked out
for his friend the part of architect, not of destroyer, in
that future ; architects, he said, were what was most
wanted in public affairs, and Italy had always lacked
them.   There is no reason to think that Cassio's sympathy had chilled, but Cavour, in his morbid state,
thought that it was so ; he imagined that what had
drawn Cassio to him " was not I, but my powerful intellectual organisation " ; and with undeserved mistrust
he did not turn to him for comfort.

He was at the nadir of his dejection when he received
a letter in a well-known handwriting, that of a woman
who had strongly attracted him four years before by
her beauty, grace, and elevation of mind.   Separation
cut short the incipient love-affair, and Cavour never
thought of renewing it.   With the woman it was otherwise ; from her first meeting with the youth of twenty
to the day of her death, absent or present, he was the
object of an idolatry in which all her faculties united :
her being was penetrated by a self-sustaining passion

which could not cease till it had consumed her. De Stendhal is the only novelist who could have drawn such a character. She was of noble birth, and from an early age had been eminently unhappy. Cavour, in his private papers, called her "L'Inconnue," and so she will be remembered. Her own life-story, and whether she was free to give her heart where she would, the world does not and need not know; on the last point it is enough to say that Cavour's father and mother were aware of his relations with her and saw in them nothing reprehensible.

On a page meant for no eyes but his own, Cavour describes the excitement into which he was thrown by the brief letter which announced that the Unknown had arrived at Turin and that she wished to see him. He hastened back to town and sought her at her hotel, and then at the opera where she had gone. After looking all round the house, he recognised her in a box—the sixth to the left on the first row—dressed in deep mourning and showing on her face such evident marks of suffering that he was at once filled with remorse "and intoxicated by a love so pure, so constant, and so disinterested." Never would he forsake this divine woman again!

For a moment he thought of flight to distant shores, but he soon decided that "imperative duties required that she should remain where she was." Their intercourse chiefly consisted of letters; his do not seem to exist, hers were found after his death carefully preserved and numbered. In these letters she laid bare her innermost soul; she was ardently patriotic, steeped in the Ideas of Mazzini, and far more Italian than Piedmontese,

though she wrote in French. She knew English, and
Cavour advised her to read Shakespeare. Remarkably
gifted, she had the deep humility of many of the best
Italian women; "What have I done, O Camille," she
asks, "to meet a soul like yours! . . . To have known
you for an instant fills a long existence; how can you
love me, weak as I am?" She had an astonishing
instinct of his future greatness: "Full of force, life,
talent, called, perhaps to make a brilliant career, to
contribute to the general good," such expressions as these
occur frequently in her letters. The romance ended as
it could not help ending. The "eternal vows" were
kept for a year and a few months; then on Cavour's
side a love which, though he did not guess it, had only
been a reflection, faded into compassionate interest.
The *Inconnue* uttered no reproaches; after a few unhappy
years she died, leaving a last letter to her inconstant
lover. "The woman who loved you is dead . . . no
one ever loved you as she did, no one! For, O Camille,
you never fathomed the extent of her love." With a
broken-hearted pride she declared that "in the domain
of death she surpassed all rivals." It remained true; if
Cavour was not, strictly speaking, more faithful to the
Inconnue's memory than he had been to her while she
lived, yet this was the only real love-passage in his life.
Fatal to her, it was fortunate to him. It found him in
despair and it left him self-reliant and matured. The
love of such a woman was a liberal education.

CHAPTER II

TRAVEL-YEARS

DURING the fifteen years which he devoted to agriculture, Cavour made several long and important visits to France and England. In this way he enlarged his experience, while keeping aloof from the governing class in his own country, connection with which could, in his opinion, only bring loss of reputation and effacement in the better days that were to come. Cavour knew himself to be ambitious, but he had the self-control never even to contemplate the purchase of what then passed for power by the sacrifice of his principles. "My principles," he once wrote, "are a part of myself." The best way "to prepare for the honourable offices of the future" was to keep his independence intact, and to study abroad the working of the institutions which he wished to see introduced at home. Through his French relations, he took his place immediately in the best society of the capital of the citizen king, under whose reign, sordid as it was in some respects, Paris attained an intellectual brilliancy the like of which was never equalled in the spectacular glare of the second empire. It was the moment of a short-lived renaissance ; literature, art, science, seemed to be start-

ing on new voyages of discovery. New worlds were
opened up for conquest; oriental studies for the first
time became popular, the great field of unwritten traditions surrendered its virgin soil. Above all, it was a
time of fermentation in moral ideas; every one expected
the millennium, though there was a lack of agreement
as to what it would consist in. Every one, like Lamennais
in Béranger's poem, was going "to save the world."
The Good, the True, the Beautiful, were about to dislodge
the Bad, the False, the Ugly. If all these high hopes
had some fruition in the region of thought, they had
none in the region of facts, but meanwhile they lent a
rare charm to Paris in the Thirties. Cavour speaks of
elasticity as the ruling quality of French society; he
praises the admirable union of science and wit, depth
and amiability, substance and form, to be found in
certain Parisian salons and nowhere else. He was thinking especially of the salon of Mme. de Circourt, who became his friend through life. For no one else had he
quite the same unchanging regard. Attracted as he
always was by the conquest of difficulties, he admired
the force of mind and will by which this Russian lady,
whom a terrible accident had made a hopeless invalid,
overcame disabilities that would have reduced most
people to a state of living death. In her, spirit an-
nihilated matter. She joined French vivacity to the
penetrating sensibility of the Sclavonic races, and she
was a keen reader of character. Cavour interested her
at once. Even in his exterior, the young Italian, with
blond hair and blue eyes, was then more attractive than
those who only knew the Cavour of later years could
easily believe; while his gay and winning manners,

combined with a fund of information on subjects not
usually popular with the young, could not but strike so
discerning a judge as the Countess de Circourt as indi-
cating not a common personality. She feared lest so
much talent and promise would be suffocated for ever
in the stifling air of a small despotism. Cavour himself
drew a miserable picture of his country : science and
intelligence were reputed "infernal things by those
who are obliging enough to govern us"; a triumphant
bigotry trembled alike at railways and Rosmini ; Cavour's
aunt, the Duchess de Clermont Tonnerre, only got per-
mission to receive the *Journal des Débats* after long
negotiations between the French minister at Turin and
the Sardinian government. No wonder if Mme. de
Circourt impulsively entreated the young man to shake
the dust of Piedmont off his feet and to seek a career in
France. In his answer to this proposition, he asks first
of all, what have his parents done that he should plunge
a knife into their hearts ? Sacred duties bound him to
them, and he would never quit them till they were
separated by the grave. This filial piety stands the
more to Cavour's credit, as his home life had not been
very happy. He went on to inquire, what real induce-
ment was there for him to abandon his native land ?
A literary reputation ? Was he to run after a little
celebrity, a little glory, without ever reaching the real
goal of his ambition ? What influence could he exercise
in favour of his unhappy brothers in a country where
egotism monopolised the high places ? What was the
mass of foreigners doing which had been thrown into
Paris by choice or misfortune ? Who among them was
useful to his fellow-men ? The political troubles which

desolated Italy had obliged her noblest sons to fly far
from her, but in their exile their eminent faculties became forceless and sterile.   Only one Italian had made
a name in Paris, Pellegrino Rossi ; but this man, whose
capacities Cavour rated as extraordinary, reached the
summit of success open to him in France when he
obtained a professorship at the Sorbonne and a chair
in the Academy, whereas, in the country which he
repudiated, he might have one day guided his com-
patriots in the paths of the new civilisation—words
which read like an imperfect prophecy, since the unfortunate Rossi was to lose his life later in the attempt
to reform the papal government.   Cavour repeats that
literature would be the only promising opening, and for
literature he feels no vocation ; he has a reasoning, not
an inventive head ; he does not possess a grain of
imagination ; in his whole life he had never been able
to construct even the smallest story to amuse a child ; at
best he would be a third-class literary man, and he says
in the matter of art he can only conceive one position :
the highest.   Certainly he might turn to science ; to
become a great mathematician, chemist, physicist, was a
way of seeking glory as good as another; only he con-
fessed that it had few attractions "for the Italian with
the rosy complexion and the smile of a child."   Ethical
science interested him more, but this was to be pursued
in retirement, not in great cities.   "No, no," he writes,
"it is not in flying from one's fatherland because it is
unhappy that one can attain a glorious end."   But if
he were mistaken, if a splendid future awaited him on
foreign soil, still his resolution would be the same.
Evil be to him who denies his fellow-countrymen as

unworthy of him. "Happy or unhappy, my country shall have all my life; I will never be unfaithful to her even were I sure of finding elsewhere a brilliant destiny."

While Cavour was in Paris, Tocqueville's *Democracy in America* was published, and immediately gave its author European fame. It did not probably exercise much influence over Cavour in the formation of opinions, but he found his own confirmed in it both as to the tendency of modern societies towards democracy for better or worse, and also as to the independence of the Church from State control, in which, from the time that he began to think at all on such matters, he had thought to see the solution of all difficulties of a politico-religious sort. Cavour changed his practice, but rarely his mind; most of the conclusions of the statesman had been reached at twenty-five. It was not easy for him to take those who fundamentally differed from him entirely seriously. Once, when he was the guest of the Princess Belgiojoso, Musset's irresponsive idol and Heine's good angel, the fair hostess bestowed on him such a republican lecture that he wrote, "They will not catch me there again"; but he went. At the Duchess d'Abrantés' receptions he met "the relics of all the governments." He only spoke on one occasion to Guizot. The minister seems to have received him coldly. He remarked that with these great people you must be a person of import-ance to make any way; an obscure citizen of Piedmont, unknown beyond the commune of which he was syndic, could have no chance. With Thiers he got on much better; principles apart, their temperaments were not inharmonious. Of the literary men Cavour preferred

Sainte Beuve; in Cousin he cared less for the philosopher than for the friend of Santorre di Santa Rosa,
the exiled patriot of 1821.   Cousin introduced him to
several fervid Italian liberals, among others Berchet, the
poet.   He was invited by Alessandro Bixio to meet the
author of *Monte Cristo*.   Bixio was one day to be
intimately mixed up in Franco-Italian politics, in which
he acted as intermediary between Cavour and Prince
Napoleon.   Royer Collard, Jules Simon, Michelet,
Ozanum, Quinet, and the Polish poet Adam Mickiewicz
were then giving lectures, which Cavour found time to
attend.   The great Rachel filled the stage.   Cavour,
who in his later years never went to a theatre except
when he wanted to go to sleep, was a warm admirer of
the incomparable actress, who satisfied his requirement
of the absolutely first class in art.   He was drawn to
the highest genius as much as he was repelled by
mediocrity.   He blamed Rachel, however, for the choice
of one particularly repulsive *rôle*, and suspected that she
chose it because the dress suited her to perfection.

It was always known that Cavour staked considerable
sums at cards, but that he had at one time a real
passion for gambling was hardly supposed till the self-
accusations of his journal were laid bare.   Though there
was little in him of the Calvinism of his maternal
ancestors, he judged himself on this point with the
severity of an austere moralist.   In the world of pleasure
in which he moved such offences were considered venial,
but he looked upon them with the disgust of a man who
reckons personal freedom beyond all earthly goods, and
who sees himself in danger of becoming a slave.   "The
humiliating and degrading emotions of play" threaten,

he says, to undermine his intellectual and moral faculties; his "miserable weakness" degrades him in his own eyes; conscience, reason, self-respect, interest, call upon him to fight against it and destroy it. From high play at cards to gambling on the Bourse there is but a step. Cavour embarked in a speculation the success of which depended on the outbreak of war in the East, which he believed to be imminent. No war occurred, and the loss of a few hundred pounds obliged him to apply to his father for supplies. The Marquis sent the money, and wrote good-naturedly that the mishap might teach Camille to moderate his belief in his own infallibility. He thought himself the only young man in the world in whom there was a ready-made minister, banker, manufacturer, and speculator; and if he did not take care the idea that he could never be wrong might prevent him from turning to account the superior gifts with which he was undoubtedly endowed. But the kindliness of the reproof did not lessen his own sense of shame and mortification. The lesson was useful; he forsook the Bourse, and at cards he conquered the passion without giving up the game. Rightly or wrongly it was said that many years after he played high stakes at whist with political men to gain an insight into their characters. In any case there is nothing to show that his fondness for play ever again led him into excesses which his judgment condemned. He had recovered his freedom.

Cavour invariably ended his visits to Paris by crossing the Channel, and, if in the French capital he gained greater knowledge of men, it was in England that he first grew familiar with the public life which he considered a pattern for the world. He did not find the delightful social intercourse to be enjoyed in Paris; in fact, not one of the persons to whom he brought letters of introduction took the least notice of him. English society is quicker to run after celebrities than to discern them in embryo. But the two or three Englishmen whom he already knew were active in his behalf. William Brockedon, his old friend, the painter, conducted him to the dinner of the Royal Geographical Society, where a curious thing happened. Cavour's first essay in public speaking was before an English assembly. After several toasts had been duly honoured, the Secretary of the Society, to his unbounded astonishment, proposed his health. Taken unawares, he expressed his thanks in a few words, which were well received, and on sitting down he said to his neighbour, the Earl of Ripon, "C'est mon *maiden speech !*" Lord Ripon remarked, "with a significant smile," that he hoped it would be the opening of a long career. He dined with John Murray, and went to see Faraday, who in his working clothes made him think of a philosopher of the sixteenth century. At a party given by Babbage, the mathematician, he met Hallam, Tocqueville, Ada Byron, and the three beautiful daughters of Sheridan. With Nassau Senior he began a long friendship, and Edward Romilly, the librarian of Trinity College, Cambridge, whom he had met at Geneva, introduced him to a rich landed proprietor of the name of Davenport, who was to prove the most useful of all his English acquaintances, as he liberally placed his house in Cheshire at Cavour's disposal to give him an opportunity of studying English agriculture. The chance was not thrown away. Cavour learnt everything about the management of a well-ordered English estate down to the minutest particulars. He admired much, especially the system of subsoil drainage, then a novelty to foreigners, but he was not carried away by the beautiful appearance of the English country so far as to think that the English farmer was in all respects ahead of the North Italian. He compared the up-and-down English meadow left to itself with the highly-manured pasture lands of Piedmont, level as billiard-boards, which yield their three crops of hay a year. One point Cavour was never tired of impressing on students of agriculture; it was this, and it exactly shows his habit of mind : never consider results without knowing what they cost. Correct the selling price by the cost of production. He had no patience with model farms ; they might be magnificent, but they were not agriculture. In one of his earliest writings he held them up to ridicule.

In England he studied the then new Poor Laws ; even before he started on his first travels, he decided to inquire into the position of the poorest classes in the countries he visited. He recognised that the acknow-ledgment of the prescriptive right of every member of the community to food and shelter was the first step to vast changes in social legislation. Cavour's natural inclinations were more those of a social and economic reformer than of the political innovator. Gasworks, factories, hospitals, and prisons were in turn inspected. Cavour went thoroughly into the questions of prison labour and diet. He did not object to the treadmill in itself, but thought unfruitful labour demoralising. Useful work with a small gain reformed the convict. The

prison fare seemed to him rather too good. He was
impressed by the bread "as good as the best that is
consumed in the clubs." Probably, next to the police-
man, what impresses the thinking foreigner most in the
British Isles is the Englishman's loaf of white bread. It
might appear that in his close study of utilitarian England, Cavour missed the greater England of imagination
and adventure, of genius and energy. It is true that he
did homage at the shrine of Shakespeare by a visit to
Stratford-on-Avon, and that he declared that there was no
sight in the world equal to the Life Guards on their
superb black horses. But his real appreciation of the
greatness of England is not to be looked for in the
jottings of the tourist; it stands forth conspicuously in
his few but singularly weighty early political writings.
The English politician whom he most admired was Pitt.
The preference was striking in a young man who was
considered a dangerous liberal in his own country. It
showed amongst other things an adoption of an English
standpoint in appraising English policy which is rare in
a foreigner. "In attacking France," Cavour wrote,
"Pitt preserved social order in England, and kept civilisation in the paths of that regular and gradual progress
which it has followed ever since." He said of him:
"He loved power not as an end but as a means"—
words which long after he applied to himself: "You
know that I care nothing for power as power; I care
for it only as a means to compass the good of my
country."

Cavour had the cast of mind which admires in others
its own qualities. As he revered Pitt's "vast and
puissant intelligence," so he sympathised with Peel's

logic and courage. Peel was his favourite among his contemporaries ; he called him " the statesman who more than any other had the instinct of the necessity of the moment." He foretold Peel's abolition of the Corn Laws at a time when no one else anticipated it. When he himself was charged by his old friends in the Turin Chamber with desertion and treason, he reminded them that the same charges had been made against Peel, but that he was largely compensated by the knowledge that he had saved England from socialist commotions, which in that country were in reality even more threatening in their scope and extent than in the rest of agitated Europe. He used to say that if Pitt had lived in times of peace he would have been a reformer after the fashion of Peel and Canning, adding his own venturesomeness to the largeness of views of the one and the capable sound sense of the other.

These scattered judgments are drawn from the essays written by Cavour in the years 1843-46. They appeared in Swiss or French reviews at a period when it was easier to make a reputation by a magazine article than it is now. Cavour's monographs attracted attention by the writer's display of independent thought and first-hand information. The most interesting now is that on " the condition and future of Ireland," which has been often referred to in the British Parliament. Most of the suggestions made in it have been long since carried into effect, but it is not these that make the essay still worth reading : it is Cavour's mode of approaching the question. He writes as what has been lately called an " Imperialist," though it was formerly thought enough to say " Englishman." It is doubtful if any foreign publicist ever wrote in the same spirit on the relations of England and Ireland either before or since. It is only necessary to be familiar with the continental press, from Legitimist to Socialist, to know, what he knew himself, that Cavour was almost in a minority of one. He was not acquainted with a single English politician ; no one influenced him ; he judged the Irish question from the study of history past and present, and having formed an unpopular opinion, he was prepared to stand by it. He never held that politics are a game of chance ; he believed that they are subject to fixed laws of cause and effect, and he worked out political problems by seeking and applying these laws to the case in point without passion or prejudice. Having satisfied himself that the union of Ireland and England was for the good of both, he was not disposed to quarrel with the means by which it was accomplished. When Pitt failed to carry the Bill for the Union through the Irish House of Commons, he resorted to the expedient, " which had never failed in the Dublin Parliament," of corruption on a large scale. He bought rotten boroughs ; he was prodigal of places, honours, pensions, and at the end of a year he obtained a majority of 168 votes against 73. Was he wrong ? Cavour thought not, though he found no words strong enough to condemn the men who sold their conscience for place or gold. Public opinion, he said, has always sanctioned in governments the use of a different morality from that binding on individuals. In all ages an extreme indulgence has been shown towards immoral acts which brought about great political results. He conceded, for the sake of argument, that such indulgence might be a fatal error ; but he insisted that if

Pitt's character was to be blackened because he used parliamentary corruption, the same censure ought in justice to be extended to the greatest monarchs of past times, Louis XIV., Joseph II., Frederic the Great, who, to serve their own ends, outraged the immovable principles of humanity and morality in a far graver manner than could be laid to the charge of the illustrious statesman who consolidated the United Kingdom of Great Britain and Ireland.

On Cavour's own grounds, those of expediency, it might be objected that a bargain which on one side you allow to be discreditable leaves the legacy of an indestructible desire on that side to wipe out the discredit by tearing it up. Though Cavour became great by his connection with a movement which, before all things, was swayed by sentiment, he never entirely recognised the part that sentiment plays in politics. He blamed O'Connell for demanding repeal, which, even if possible to obtain, would do as much harm to Ireland as to England, instead of supporting measures that would remove all cause for Irish discontent. Had he lived long enough he would have seen all those measures passed, but he would not have seen the end to Irish discontent. This might have surprised him, but not so much as to see a great English party advocating disunion, which, he declared, could be logically supported only "by those who thought it desirable that there should be a revolution."

Cavour noticed and deplored the unpopularity of England on the Continent. Extreme parties, opposed in everything else, were agreed in a violent hatred of that country. The moderate party liked it in theory,

but in reality they had no natural sympathy with it.
Only a few individuals who rose superior to the passions
of the multitude felt the esteem due to a nation which
had powerfully contributed to develop the moral and
material resources of the world, and whose mission was
far from ended. The masses were almost everywhere
hostile to it. It was a mistake to suppose that this was
the feeling of France alone ; it might be expressed more
loudly there, but it was, in fact, universal. The enemies
of progress and the partisans of political subversion
looked on England as their worst adversary : the former
charged her with being the hotbed of revolutionary
propagandism ; the latter, perhaps with more reason,
considered the English aristocracy as the corner-stone of
the social edifice of Europe. England ought to be
popular with the friends of gradual reform and regular
progress, but a host of prejudices, recollections, passions,
produced the contrary effect. With but little alteration
the lines here condensed might have been written
to-day.

A book on railways by Count Petitti had been prohibited in Piedmont. That railways were connected
with the Powers of Darkness was then a general opinion,
shared in particular by Pope Gregory. Cavour reviewed
the book in the *Revue nouvelle*, which was also prohibited,
but sundry copies of it were smuggled into Italy, and
one even reached the king. While Petitti had avoided
all political allusions, Cavour's article abounds in them :
railways would promote the moral union of Italy, which
must precede the conquest of national independence.
Municipal jealousies, intellectual backwardness, would
disappear, and, when that happened, nothing could

prevent the accomplishment of the object which was the passionate desire of all—emancipation. A very small number of ideas forms the intellectual hinge of man in the aggregate; of these patriotism is only second in importance to religion. Any conception of national dignity in the masses was impossible without the pride of nationality. Every private interest, every political dissension, should be laid aside that Italian independence might become a fact. Cavour always spoke of Italy— not of Piedmont, not of Lombardy and Venetia. Rome, still of all cities the richest in precious memories and splendid hopes, would be the centre of an iron network uniting the whole peninsula. Some well-intentioned patriots objected to the increase of railway communication with Austria from the fear that it would strengthen her military and political hold over her Italian provinces. Cavour answered that the great events at hand could not be delayed by the shortening of the number of hours between Vienna and Milan. On the other hand, when the relations arising out of conquest were replaced by those of friendship and equity, rapid communication would promote the moral and intellectual intercourse, "which, more than any one, we desire," between grave and profound Germany and intelligent Italy. In these pages Cavour foreshadowed the boring of the Alps and the German alliance, two facts which then seemed equally improbable.

The man was made; he waited for his opportunity. What if it never came? Can we conceive Cavour's immense energy limited to a rice-field? Are there really men whom their lot forbids—

> Th' applause of list'ning senates to command,
>   The threats of pain and ruin to despise,
> To scatter plenty o'er a smiling land,
>   And read their hist'ry in a nation's eyes?

The prophet may cry aloud in the desert, the scientific discoverer may guess at truths which his age rejects, but the total waste of such a force as the mind of Cavour seems less easy to imagine than that his appearance was a sign that the times were ripe for him.

CHAPTER III

In 1846, Cavour was only known at home as the most unpopular man in Piedmont. Most people can scarcely be said to be unpopular before they have occupied any public position, but this, strangely enough, was the case with Cavour. He was simply a private person, but he was hated by all parties. His writings, which had made their mark abroad, were little known in Italy; the reviews in which they appeared could only be obtained by stealth. No one rightly knew what his views were, but every one disliked him. Solaro de la Margherita, the retrograde prime minister, was detested by the liberals, but he had a strong following among the old Savoyard nobility; Lorenzo Valerio, the radical manufacturer, was harassed by those in power, but he was adored by the people; Cavour was in worse odour with both parties than these two men were with either. Under the porticoes of Turin petty private talk took the place of anything like public discussion. "By good fortune," as the prime minister put it, "the press was not free in Piedmont;" quite the reverse. Gossip, especially spiteful gossip, reigned supreme. Gossip in both spheres of society was all against Cavour. What might be called the Court party (though whether the king belonged to it or it to the king was not clear), with the tenacious memory of small coteries, still recollected Cavour as the self-willed student of the Military Academy. Charles Albert himself made an occasional polite inquiry of the Marquis as to his son's travels and his visits to prisons and hospitals, but, unless report erred, he was speaking of him to others as the most dangerous man in his kingdom. The degree to which Cavour was hated by the conservatives is shown by one small fact: he was treasurer of an Infant Asylum, but it was thought necessary privately to ask him to retire for the good of the charity, his connection with which set all the higher society against it. The case with the radicals was no better. He belonged to an agricultural association in which Valerio was a leading spirit; one day he asked leave to speak, upon which almost all the members present left the building. On this side, no doubt part of the antipathy arose from the popular feeling against Cavour's father, who still occupied the invidious and ill-defined office of Vicario. No particular ferocity was laid at his door, but he was supposed to serve up all the private affairs of the good Turinese to the king, and if any one got into trouble he was thought to be the cause. When the liberals triumphed, the first thing they did was to oblige him to resign. Then Cavour's elder brother, though not retrograde on economic subjects, was a conservative of the old school in politics. In later days Gustavo always voted against Camillo. In politics the brothers were in admirable agreement to differ; in fact, after the first trifling jars, they dwelt to the end in unruffled harmony in the family palace, Via dell' Arcivescovado. At the time when Gustavo was much better known at Turin than Camillo the suspicious radical could not persuade himself that one brother was not as much of an aristocrat as the other. When Mr. Cobden was cordially received by both Marquis and Count, a would-be wit exclaimed, "There goes Free-trade in the charge of Monopoly," which was understood to refer to the false accusation that the Cavours had stored up a quantity of grain in that year of scarcity, 1847, in order to sell it dear, the truth being simply that the improved cultivation introduced at Leri had secured fair crops in a bad season.

The festivities in honour of the English Free-trader were promoted all over Italy by Italians who were soon to become famous. The fact that Cobden was an Englishman, even more than the outwardly harmless object of his campaign, deterred the different governments from interfering with him. Cavour proposed the health of the guest of the evening at the Cobden banquet at Turin, but almost immediately after, he retired to Leri, as he did not wish it to appear that he meant to embark on public life while the existing political dead-lock lasted. There was only room for conspirators or for those who extended toleration to the *régime* in force. It is doubtful if anything would have driven Cavour to conspiracy against his own king, and he would have considered it a personal disgrace to be mixed up with the men then in power. He thought, therefore, that he could best serve his country by keeping himself in reserve. He realised the futility of small concessions, and the childishness of agitating to obtain them. He was the only strong

royalist who understood how far reform must go when
it once began—farther towards democracy than his own
sympathies would have carried him. If you want to
use a mill-stream you must let it flow.

The situation in Piedmont was briefly this : Charles
Albert's heart was with the growing cry for independence, but he wished for independence without liberty.
This was the "secret of the king" which has been
sought for in all kinds of recondite suppositions : this
was the key to his apparently vacillating and inconsistent
character. Yet he revealed it himself in some words
spoken to Roberto d' Azeglio, the elder brother of
Massimo. "Marquis d' Azeglio," he said, "I desire as
much as you do the enfranchisement of Italy, and it is
for that reason, remember well, that I will never give a
constitution to my people." While his government was
a priestly despotism, he employed his leisure in trans-
lating the sublime appeals to national sentiment in the
history of the Maccabees, of which, by a curious coin-
cidence, Mazzini once said that it seemed written for
Italians. Charles Albert made the mistake of forgetting
the age in which he lived. His ancestors fought the
stranger without troubling themselves about representative government—why should not he ? But his ancestors
represented in their own persons the nerve and sinew of the
State, its most adventurous spirit, its strongest manhood,
whereas Charles Albert represented only the party of
reaction which was with him in his absolutism but not
in his patriotism. He was accused of having changed
sides, but, even allowing his complicity in the movement
of 1821 to have been greater than he admitted, it is
plain that the one thing which drew him into that move-

ment was its championship of Italian independence. Unlike the Neapolitan revolutionists who disclaimed adventures for the freeing of Italy, at least till they had made sure of their own freedom, the liberals of Piedmont rose with the avowed purpose of rushing into an immediate war with Austria. A madder scheme was never devised, but the madness of one day is often the wisdom of the next. In politics really disinterested acts bear fruit, whatever be their consequences to individuals.

The question which agitated all minds in 1847 was whether or not Charles Albert could be gained to the liberal cause. Many despaired, for by many even his Italian ambition was denied. Cavour had no favourable opinion of the king, but it was one of his theories that erroneous ideas always yield in the end to facts. He believed that Charles Albert's support could be secured if he were fully persuaded that the interests of his dynasty were not imperilled. He was not afraid, as others were, that even after the first surrender the wavering mind of the king would make retrogression probable; he understood that, if reforms were more difficult to obtain in Piedmont than elsewhere, they would be more durable when obtained. At last a concession of real value was wrung from the king : the censure was revoked. Cavour saw that the press, which till then had been a cipher, would instantly become of vast importance. He left his retirement to found a newspaper, to which he gave the name by which the Italian movement will be known in history—*Il Risorgimento*. He was not a born journalist, but he set himself with his usual determination to learn the art. In

after times he said that the experience gained in a newspaper office was almost as profitable to him as the knowledge of mathematics. Count Cesare Balbo was asked
by Cavour to write the prospectus of the new journal,
in which its aims were described as Independence, union
between the princes and people, and reforms. Cavour's
name appeared as acting and responsible editor.

Balbo's work, *Le Speranze d' Italia*, had lately created
an impression, only second to that made by the Primato
of Gioberti. Practical men like Cavour preferred the
simple programme which Balbo put forward—the liberation of Italy from foreign yoke before all things—to
Gioberti's mystical outpourings, much as they pleased
the general. Gioberti, once a follower of Mazzini, and
afterwards a priest, imagined a United Italy, with the
Pope at its head, which, to unthinking souls, seemed to
be on the road to miraculous realisation when the amiable
and popular Cardinal Mastai Feretti was invested with
the tiara. Cavour never had any hope in the Papacy
as a political institution.

The Genoese, impatient of the extreme slowness with
which reforms were meted out, proposed to send a
deputation with a petition for a civic guard, and the
expulsion of the Jesuits, to whom the delay was attributed, and who were regarded as the worst enemies
of the liberal Pope. The principal editors, with other
influential citizens of Turin, met at the Hôtel d'Europe
to consider how the deputation should be received, and
if their demands were to be supported. The list of the
journalists present comprises the best names in the
country ; it would be difficult to find more distinguished
or disinterested pressmen than those who were then

writing for the Piedmontese newspapers. Valerio was there to represent his new journal, *Concordia*, in which he carried on war to the knife with Cavour. His high personal character, as well as his talents, made him no inconsiderable opponent. It was at this meeting that Cavour first entirely revealed himself. He showed that faith in *the prudence of daring* which was the keynote to his great strokes of policy. The demands of the Genoese, he said, were not too large, but too small. They hit wide of the mark, and the second of them was idle, because the king, while he remained an absolute prince, was certain not to consent to it. The government was now neither one thing nor the other; it had lost the authority of an autocracy, and had not gained that of a *régime* based on the popular will. The situation was intolerable and dangerous; what was wanted was not this or that reform, but a constitution.

Constitutions seem tame to us now, but to speak of a constitution at Turin on January 18, 1848, was almost as audacious as it would be to speak of it at St. Petersburg at the present time. Europe stood at the brink of a precipice, but knew it not. The news had only just spread of the first symptom of revolution—the rising in Sicily. Cavour's speech was a moral bomb-shell. Most politicians begin by asking for more or less than the measure which finally contents them; those who cried for a republic have been known to put up with a limited monarchy; those who preached the most moderate reforms, at a later stage have danced round trees of liberty. Cavour asked at once for what he wanted and all that he wanted as far as the internal organisation of the State was concerned. From first to last he believed that a

constitutional monarchy was the only form of government which, in a country like Italy, could combine freedom
with order.   Under no narrower system would he accept
office, and when in office nothing could make him untrue
to his constitutional faith ; "no state of siege" was the
axiom of his political life.

How his proposal was received shows the difficulties
with which he had to contend from the outset. The more
moderate members of the meeting thought that he had
taken leave of his senses.   This was natural.   Less
natural was the tooth and nail opposition of Valerio,
who declared that a constitution much exceeded the
desires of the people, and that a petition for it would
only frighten the king.   He carried all the radicals with
him except Brofferio, an honest patriot and the writer
of charming poems in the Piedmontese dialect, which
gave him a great popularity.   Brofferio was an ultra-
democrat, but he was no party man, and he had the
courage to walk over to the unpopular editor of the
Risorgimento with the remark, "I shall always be with
those who ask the most." Valerio made no secret among
his private friends of the real reasons of his conduct.
What was the good of wasting efforts on some sort of
English constitution, perhaps with a House of Lords
and other such abominations?   Was it likely that anything worth having would be excogitated by Milord
Camillo, the greatest reactionary in the kingdom, the
sworn foe of revolution, "un Anglomane pur sang?"
A constitution could only check the revolution and
stifle the legitimate aspirations of the people.   The
nickname of "Milord Camillo" or "Milord *Risorgimento*" was in every one's mouth when speaking of Cavour.

A short time sufficed to show not only the expediency
but the necessity of granting a constitution, and that at
once.   Events never moved so fast as in the first two
months of 1848.   The throne of Louis Philippe was
tottering, and, with the exception of the Duke of Modena,
the princelings of Italy snatched the plank of safety of
a statute with the alacrity of drowning men.   In this
crisis Charles Albert thought of abdication.   Besides
the known causes of his hesitancy, there was one then
unknown : the formal engagement, invented by Metternich and forced upon him by his uncle Charles Felix, to
govern the country as he found it governed.   He called
the members of the royal family together and informed
them that if there must be a constitution there must,
but the decree which bestowed it would be signed by
his son.   The queen and the Duchess of Savoy, who
were both extremely afraid of him, sat in silence ; the
handsome Duke of Genoa tried to prove that constitutions were not such dreadful things ; Victor Emmanuel
opposed his intention of abdicating in resolute terms.
Then he summoned a high ecclesiastic, who succeeded in
convincing him that it would be a greater sin to abandon
his people in their need than to break a promise he
could no longer maintain.   After mortifying the flesh
with fasts and vigils, he yielded, and the famous decree
bore the signature " C. Alberto " after all,—not written
indeed in the king's usually beautiful character, but
betraying rather a trembling hand, which nevertheless registered a great because a permanent fact.
This was not the prelude to perjury and expulsion.
Around the Sardinian statute were united the
scattered limbs of Italy, and after fifty years Charles

Albert's grandson commemorated its promulgation at the Capitol.

Not a man in the crowd at Turin dared to anticipate such a result : yet their joy was frantic. Fifty thousand people, arranged in guilds, defiled before the king, who sat like a statue on his bay horse, upright and impassible. Cavour walked in the company of journalists, and all those who had opposed him a few weeks before were there too, with Valerio at their head. They sang their strophe of Mameli's hymn, "Fratelli d' Italia," very badly. Cavour whispered to his neighbour, " We are so many dogs ! "

That neighbour, a Milanese named Giuseppe Torelli, has left an interesting description of Cavour's appearance as it was then. He was fresh-coloured, and his blue eyes had not yet lost their brightness, but they were so changeful in expression that it was difficult to fix their distinctive quality. Though rather stout he was not ungainly, as he tended to become later. He stooped a little, and two narrow lines were visible on either side of a mouth, cold and uneffusive ; but these lines, by their trembling or contraction, showed the play of inward emotion which the rest of the face concealed. In after days people used to watch them in order to guess his state of mind. It was his large and solid forehead that chiefly gave the idea of power which every one who saw him carried away, despite of the want of dignity in his person and of strongly-marked features in his face. His manners were simple, but distinguished by an unmistakably aristocratic ease and courtesy. He spoke generally low and without emphasis, and always appeared to pay great attention to what was said to him, even by the least important person.

Nothing, on the face of it, could seem more extraordinary than the exclusion of Cavour from office in the
momentous year of 1848.   But he had no popular party
at his back whose cry could overrule the disinclination
which the king certainly felt towards making him his
Minister.   Moreover, his abilities, though now generally
recognised, contributed to keeping him in the background : it was felt instinctively that if he got the reins
there would be only one driver.   He was known to be
indifferent to criticism, and while he listened patiently
to advice, he rarely took it.   He had mortally offended
the conservatives by the liberalism of his means, and
the liberals by the conservatism of his ends.   Count
Balbo, on assuming the office of the first Prime Minister
under the Statute, not only retired from the directing
council of the *Risorgimento*, but went out of his way to
disavow the policy supported in it by Cavour.   "The
little rascal," he was heard to say, " will end by ruining
the splendid edifice raised by the wisdom and moderation of so many estimable men !"   The splendid
edifice was on the verge of being nearly ruined, but
by timidity — which has lost a score of thrones, —
not by audacity.   The new Cabinet entered upon their
duties on March 16.   Two days later occurred an event
utterly unforeseen — the rising of Milan against the
Austrians.   It took them unprepared.   They had talked
so much about war that perhaps they thought it would
happen in the next century.   When the "now or never"
sounded, which does sound sooner or later in all human
affairs, they hesitated or suffered the king to hesitate,
which came to the same thing.   That Charles Albert
stood for one instant in doubt when the hour was come

desired by him all his life, as he had often stated, and
there is no reason to think untruly, is possibly the most
serious stain on his memory.   There are moments when
to reflect is criminal : a man has no right to reflect when
his mother is in a burning house.   The reflections which
held Charles Albert back were two.   He was afraid that
the Milan revolution would breed a republic, and he
was afraid of England and of Russia.   England, which
during the previous autumn had sent Lord Minto to
urge upon the Italian princes a line of policy rightly
described by Prince Metternich as inevitably leading to
an attack on Austria, now applied the whole force of her
diplomacy to stop the ball she had herself set running.
The spectacle of Lord Palmerston trying to save or serve
Austria, which he detested, in obedience to the atavistic
tendencies of the Foreign Office, is a lesson in history.
For English politicians of whatever party or private
sentiments, Austria was still what Lord Castlereagh
called her : " The great hinge on which the fate of
Europe must ultimately depend."   Sir Ralph Abercromby
assured the king that " the least act of aggression "
would place his throne in jeopardy.   His throne was
already in jeopardy, but from the contrary reason.
Each minute that passed while the Milanese were
fighting their death struggle and he stood inactive
threatened to deprive him and his house of that power of
progress on which not only their fortune but their
existence depended.

The news from Milan reached Turin on March 19 ;
on the 23rd, the last of the Milan days, king and
ministry were still hesitating.   On that day Cavour
printed in the *Risorgimento* the most impassioned piece

of writing that ever came from his pen. The conservative, the reactionary, once more cried aloud that
audacity was prudence, temerity wisdom. The supreme
hour of the Savoy dynasty had struck, the hour of
strong resolves, on which hangs the fate of empires, the
destinies of peoples. Hesitation, doubt, delay, were no
more possible : they could only prove fatal. " We, men
of calm minds, accustomed to listen more to the dictates
of reason than to the impulses of the heart, after
deliberately weighing each word we utter, are bound in
conscience to declare that only one path is open to the
nation, the government, the king : war, immediate
war ! " It was said, he continued, that Russia and
England were on the point of uniting against Italy. In
common times such an argument would be conclusive,
not now. When Milan was struggling for life, was
perhaps getting worsted, at all costs they were bound
to fly to the rescue. Duty, brotherhood, policy, commanded it. Woe unto them if they crossed the frontier
to find that Milan had fallen.

Russia, through her ambassador, intimated that she
would regard the crossing of the Ticino as a *casus belli*.
The threat made less impression at Turin than the
warnings of Sir Ralph Abercromby ; it was the possibility of English intervention, therefore, that Cavour
went on to examine. The *Anglomane* " Milord *Risorgimento* " was less surprised at the current of English
official thought than were his radical critics, but would
any English minister, he asked, enter on a European
war to prevent the liberation of Italy, which was an
object sacred in the eyes of the mass of the English
people ? He believed it to be impossible, but were it so,

so be it! England would have against her a mighty coalition, not of princes, as in former days, but of peoples, in the old world and in the new. Victory in such a matricidal strife would be as fatal to the first-born of liberty as defeat.

Thus Cavour was prepared to fight Austria, Russia, and England. The division of parties at that time was in its essence the division of those who were willing to accept a republican solution and those who were not. It does not follow that all the liberals wished for a republic, but they would all have taken office under it. Of this there is little doubt. Cavour never would have become a republican any more than an absolutist minister. But he saw what the other conservatives failed to see, that the dynasty of Savoy could only live if it led.

On March 22, Charles Albert was still assuring the Austrian Ambassador that his intentions were pacific. Next day Cavour's article appeared, and in the evening the king decided for instant war. Only two of the ministers assented at once; the others gave in after a long discussion. War was declared on the 25th. Time lost cannot be recalled; the happy moment had been let go by; Piedmont went not to Lombardy engaged in a dangerous struggle, but to Lombardy victorious. Cavillers said that the king had come to eat the fruits others had gathered. Confidence in the ultimate result reached the point of madness, but with revolution stalking through the streets of Vienna the Austrian eagle seemed to have lost its talons. In May 1848, in Austria itself, Lombardy was looked upon as completely lost, and with it the Southern Tyrol as far as Meran, for no one at that period thought of separating this Italian district from Italy; the most sanguine Austrians only hoped to save Venetia. Radetsky alone expected to save all, because he knew what he could do, and he had judged Sardinian generalship correctly. Charles Albert's staff seemed to have but one idea—to reverse the tactics which had led the first Napoleon to victory on the same ground.

The brightest gleam of success which shone on the king of Sardinia's arms was at Goito, in the battle of May 30. It was on that occasion that Cavour's nephew, Augusto di Cavour, was killed. The *enfant terrible* grew up to be a young man of singular promise, on whom Cavour had fixed all his hopes for the future of his name and house. His uncle's last letter of encouragement to do his duty was found on Augusto's body. The blow unnerved Cavour; he was found lying prostrate in an agony of speechless grief. Through his life he kept the blood-stained uniform in which the young officer received his death-wound in a glass case in his bedroom, a piece of enduring sentiment which shows how unlike Cavour was the coldly calculating egotist whose portrait has passed for his.

The story of the years of revolution in Italy is a story of great things and small, like most human records; but, when all is said, the great predominate, for no blunders could efface the readiness for self-sacrifice displayed by the whole people. The experience of these years was bitter, but possibly necessary. It destroyed illusions. It showed, for instance, that in the nineteenth century a free and independent Italy under the hegemony of the Pope belonged to political mythology. Here was

a Pope who was, at heart, patriotic, but who drew back
at the crucial moment, precisely as Mazzini (almost
alone) had predicted. The first threat of a schism was
enough to make him wear dust and ashes for his
patriotism. The Bourbons of Naples were ascertained
to have learnt nothing and unlearnt nothing; perfidy
alone could be expected from them. It was proved that
the princes of the other states, Piedmont excepted, must
gravitate towards Austria even if they did not wish it.
All this was useful, if dearly bought, knowledge.

At the first general elections in Piedmont, Cavour
failed to obtain a seat. He told the electors in his
address that he had always desired *Italia unita e libera*,
and if "united" did not yet imply "under one king,"
the phrase was still significant. Two months later he
was elected in four divisions; probably the death of his
nephew in the interim on the field of battle modified, for
the time, his unpopularity. He took his seat for the
first college of Turin. He did not make an immediate
impression; his short stature, and still more the imperfect accent with which he spoke Italian, were not
in his favour. French was allowed in the Sardinian
Chamber, but Cavour never opened his lips in it in
Parliament. By degrees his speeches became marvels
of close reasoning, and they even soared, sometimes,
when he was deeply moved, into a kind of eloquence
superior to that of rhetoric, but the accent was never
such as would satisfy a fastidious ear. The day came,
however, when people hung with too much anxiety on
the least of his utterances for any one to notice this
defect. Cavour sat on the Right, and from the first he
horrified his colleagues on the same benches by the

enunciation of views which to them were rank heresies. They existed in a state of perpetual uneasiness as to what he might say or do next.

Cavour was not re-elected when Parliament was dissolved in January 1849; he was therefore not in the Chamber during the debates which preceded and followed the last desperate throw of Novara. A letter written by him six days after the battle shows what he thought of those events. The Conservative party, he says, which represented the great majority in the country, had been badly supported by it (an assertion as true now as then). The king threw himself into the arms of demagogues who thought that freedom and independence were to be won by phrases and proclamations. The army had been disheartened, the best officers kept inactive; twelve months' sacrifices of men and money placed them in a worse condition than before the Milan revolution. Self-love might, he concluded, warp his judgment, but he had the intimate conviction that, if he had held the reins of power, he could have saved the country without any effort of genius, and planted the Italian flag on the Styrian Alps. But his friends joined with his foes to keep him out of power, and he had passed his time in deploring faults which it would have been very easy to avoid.

Remembering what Cavour afterwards accomplished, these are words which should not be set lightly aside. Yet it is possible that the complete disaster into which Charles Albert rushed at Novara was the only thing to save the country and to lay the foundations of Italian unity. The king was more eager for war than the most unthinking democrat. Reviled by all parties, he sought the great conciliator, death. "The Italians will never trust me," he exclaimed. "My son, Victor, will be king of Italy, not I." When the death he would have chosen was denied him, he went away, a crownless exile. He could do no more.

It was necessary, as Charles Albert had seen, that the king who was to carry out the destinies of Italy should be trusted. Victor Emmanuel came to the throne with few advantages; he was unpopular, his private friends were said to be reactionaries, his brusque manners offended most people. He had practically no advisers in these critical moments, but the moral courage with which he refused the Austrian offers of lenient terms if he would repudiate the Statute and his father's word, won for him the nation's trust, which he never lost. Cavour, with all his genius, could not have made the kingdom of Italy if the Italians had doubted their king.

CHAPTER IV

THE condition of Italy, Cavour said, was worse at the
end of the year's struggle than at the beginning. Such
was the case, if the present only were looked at. When
Austria resumed her sway in Lombardy and Venetia
she resumed it by the right of the conqueror, a more
intelligible, and in a sense a more legitimate, right than
that derived from bargains and treaties in which the
population had no voice. The House of Hapsburg was
saved in Italy by one loyal servant, Radetsky, and in
Hungary by the Ban of Croatia and 200,000 Russians.
Besides the regained supremacy in the Lombardo-Veneto,
Austria was more predominant in the centre and south
than in the palmiest days of the Holy Alliance. A keen
observer might have held that she was too predominant
to be safe. Talleyrand always said that if Italy were
united under Austria she would escape from her, not
sooner or later, but in a few years. There was not
political unity, but there may almost be said to have
been moral unity. Even in Rome, in spite of the French
garrison, Austrian influence counted for much more than
French. When Victor Emmanuel gave the premiership

to Massimo d' Azeglio, Cavour remarked that he was glad of the appointment, and equally so that D' Azeglio had not asked him to be his colleague, because in the actual circumstances it seemed to him difficult or impossible to do any good. D' Azeglio could not have offered Cavour a portfolio without undoing the effect of his own appointment, by which confidence in Victor Emmanuel was confirmed. The king was not sufficiently known for it to be wise to place beside him an unpopular man, a suspected *codino*, the nickname ("pig-tail") given to reactionaries. D'Azeglio, who was really prepared to go far less far than Cavour, was almost loved even by his political enemies, a wonderful phenomenon in Italy. His patriotism had been lately sealed by the severe wound he received at Vicenza. To rigid principles he added attractive and chivalric manners, which smoothed his relations with the young king, who, if brusque himself, did not like brusqueness in others.

Cavour retired, as became his wont, to enjoy the sweetness of rural leisure at Leri : for him the sovereign remedy to political disquietude. The well-cultivated fields, the rich grass lands, in the contemplation of which he took a peaceful but lively satisfaction, restored as usual his mental equilibrium, and brought back the hopefulness of his naturally sanguine temperament. Before long he was exhorting his friends to be of good cheer ; while liberty existed in a single corner of the peninsula there was no need to despair; if Piedmont kept her institutions free from despotism and anarchy, these would be the means of working efficaciously for the regeneration of the country. To those who went to see him he said, rubbing his hands (a sure sign that he was regaining his spirits), " We shall begin again, and, profiting by past mistakes, we shall do better next time." Probably he foresaw that "next time" he would have the game in his own hands.

The king had done his part by proving his resolve to uphold the constitution, but all danger for liberty in Piedmont did not cease there. The members of the party which had ruled during the earlier years of Charles Albert's reign did not give themselves up for lost. They cherished the hope of using the constitution to overturn liberty. On the face of things, the moral to be drawn from recent history was for and not against them. They could say that the only patent consequence of the change of system was that the country had been plunged in disaster, that blood and money had been wasted with no other effect than a bankrupt exchequer, a beaten army, trade at a standstill, misery stalking through the land. This party, which was by no means weak, could reckon on the compact support of Savoy, where Italian patriotism was as scarce as true and chivalric attachment to the royal house was abundant. Above all, it had the support of the whole power of the Church, which, through its corporations and religious orders and its army of priests, exercised an influence in Piedmont unparalleled in Austria or in Spain. If the liberal institutions of the country were to be preserved, it was necessary to strike a blow at this party by weakening the arch on which it reposed. Religious toleration had been proclaimed in Piedmont as one of the first reforms, the concession having been obtained from Charles Albert by the Marquis Robert d'Azeglio, a conservative and a profoundly convinced Catholic, but a lover of justice and mercy, who esteemed it the happiest day of his life when, through his interposition, the faithful Vaudois were granted the rights of free citizens. But legislation had not yet touched the extraordinary privileges arrogated to itself by the Church. One of these, the *Foro ecclesiastico*, a special court for the judgment of ecclesiastical offenders against the common law, it was now proposed to abolish. It was a test measure—like throwing down the gauntlet. Cavour had been re-elected when the king dissolved Parliament by what is known as the Proclamation of Moncalieri, and in the debates on the *Foro ecclesiastico* for the first time he made his power felt in the Chamber. He spoke as one who had long thought out the subject and had chosen his policy : "Render unto Cæsar the things which are Cæsar's, and to God the things which are God's."

At this first stage in the long struggle the Roman curia might have settled the matter in a friendly way, but it would not. Cardinal Antonelli replied to a respectful invitation, that "the Holy Father was ready to go to the ante-chamber of the devil's house to please the king of Sardinia, but he really could not go inside." Yet, at the same date, the Archbishop of Paris (Sibour) admitted to a Piedmontese visitor that the Sardinian Government had no option under the new institutions but to establish the equality of all citizens before the law, and in Austria they were laughing at the progressive monarchy in its laborious efforts to obtain reforms carried out in the despotic empire by Joseph II. The reason that Rome refused to treat was that she thought herself strong and Sardinia weak. Writers on this period have too readily assumed that the Church, by the law of its being, must always cry "no compromise!" Of course nothing can be more erroneous. The Church has yielded as many times as it thought itself obliged to yield. What other inference can be deduced from the strange and romantic story of the suppression of the Jesuits? and, to cite only one more instance, from the deposition of bishops for extra-canonical reasons conceded by Pius VII. to the First Consul? The curia thought that Victor Emmanuel would end at Canossa, but he ended instead in the Pantheon. It should be remembered, however, that the quarrel had nothing then to do with the dispute between pope and king on the broader grounds of the possession of Rome. That dispute was still in the darkness of the future. Sardinia had not given even moral support to the Roman Republic.

In Cavour's able speech of March 7, 1850, he observed that his friends, the Liberal Conservatives, feared the erection of the priesthood into a party hostile to the State. Peace was precious, but too heavy sacrifices might be made even to it. He himself trusted that in the long run the priesthood would recognise the necessity to modern society of the union of the two great moral forces, religion and liberty. Europe was threatened with universal revolution; only large and courageous reforms could stem the tide. M. Guizot might have saved the throne of Louis Philippe had he yielded to the demand for electoral reform. Why had there been no revolution in England? Because the Duke of Wellington in 1829, Lord Grey in 1832, and Sir Robert Peel in 1846, understood the exigencies of their epoch, proving themselves thereby to be the first statesmen of the time.

Uninfluenced by the furious attacks on him as an *Anglo-mane*, Cavour took the first opportunity of reaffirming from his seat in Parliament the admiration for English methods which he had constantly expressed outside. He closed his speech by appealing to Government to persevere in its policy of large and fearless reforms, which, far from weakening the constitutional throne, would so strengthen its roots that not only would Piedmont be enabled to resist the revolutionary storm should it break around its borders, but also "gathering to itself all the living forces in Italy, it would be in a position to lead our mother-country to those high destinies whereunto she is called."

The effect of this peroration was inconceivable. Here was the first word of hope publicly uttered since the *débâcle!* People in the galleries who had seen Cavour usually silenced by clamour and howls heard the applause with astonishment, and then joined in it. All the ministers rose to shake hands with the speaker. Any other man would have become popular at once, but against Cavour prejudice was too strong for a fleeting success to remove it. From that day, however, he was listened to. He was no longer a *quantité négligeable* in the politics of Italy or of Europe.

One of the ministers, Count Pietro di Santa Rosa, died within a few months of the bill on the *Foro* becoming law, and the last sacraments were denied to him because he refused to sign a retractation of the political acts of the cabinet of which he was a member. Cavour was an old friend of Santa Rosa. He was present when he died, and he heard from the Countess the particulars of the distressing scene when the priest in the harshest manner withheld the consolations of religion from the dying man, who was a pious Catholic, but who had the strength of mind even in death not to dishonour himself and his colleagues. Cavour wrote an indignant article in the *Risorgimento* denouncing the party spite which could cause such cruel anguish under a religious cloak, and the people of Turin became so much excited that if the further indignity of a refusal of Christian burial had been resorted to, as at first seemed probable, the lives of the priests in the city would hardly have been safe. Everything seemed to point to Cavour as Santa Rosa's successor, but Massimo d'Azeglio felt nervous at taking the final step. He was encouraged to it by General La Marmora, the friend of both, who declared that "Camillo was a *gran buon diavolo*," who would grow more moderate when "with us." Cavour accepted the offered post of Minister of Agriculture and Commerce, but not without making terms. He exacted the retirement of a minister whom he considered incurably timorous, especially in ecclesiastical legislation. The point was yielded, but D'Azeglio said to La Marmora, "We are beginning badly with your. *buon diavolo*." The good Massimo got no comfort from the king: "Don't you see that this man will turn you all out?" Victor Emmanuel casually remarked, or rather he made use of a stronger idiom in his native dialect, which would not well bear translation. The king refrained from opposing the appointment, but he did not pretend that he liked it.

About that time Cavour paid a visit to the Piedmontese shore of the Lago Maggiore, where he made the acquaintance of the author of the *Promessi Sposi.* Perhaps by reason of his poetic instinct Manzoni expected great things of him from the first. "That little man promises very well," he told the poet Berchet. And he opened his heart to Cavour, telling him that dream of Italian unity which he had always cherished, but which, as he said in his old age, he kept a secret for fear of being thought a madman. They looked across the blue line of water; there, on the other side, was Austria. Had Cavour said what he thought, he would have responded, "That is the first stone to move." But he did not enter upon a discussion; he merely murmured, rubbing his hands, "We shall do something!"

To the end Cavour evoked more ready sympathy among men of the other provinces than among the Piedmontese, although these last came to repose the blind trust in him which the Duke of Wellington's soldiers reposed in their leader—a trust born of the conviction that he would lead to victory. Latterly this was Victor Emmanuel's own way of feeling towards Cavour. Sympathy was always lacking.

On taking office Cavour sold his shares in the agricultural and industrial speculations which he had promoted, with the exception of one company, then not in a flourishing state, and likely to collapse if he withdrew his name. He also severed his connection with the *Risorgimento*, which had cost him much money and made him many enemies, but he believed that the services rendered by it to the cause of orderly liberty were incalculable. He never regretted his years of work in the *antro*, the wild beasts' den, as the advanced liberals called the office of the journal, a name gaily adopted by himself. As editor of the *Risorgimento* he fought his one duel; a scandalous attack on the personal honesty of the writers was made by a Jewish financier in an obscure Nizzard sheet; an encounter with pistols followed in which no one was hurt, but both sides seemed to have aimed in earnest. There is a tragic absurdity in the possible extinction of such a life as Cavour's on so paltry an occasion; yet, in the surroundings in which he moved, he could not have passed over the worthless attack in the silent contempt it deserved without being called a coward. At the conclusion of the duel he walked away, turning his back on his adversary, but no long time elapsed before, as minister, he was taking trouble to obtain for this man some honorific bauble which his vanity coveted.

On taking office, Cavour doubted for a moment his own future, the doubt common to men who reach a position they have waited for too long. In these times, he wrote, politicians were soon used up; probably it would be so with him. But the work of his department dispelled gloomy thoughts: as Minister of Commerce he negotiated treaties with France, England, and Belgium in which a step was made towards realising his favourite theories on free trade. Before long he was also made Minister of the Marine; it was taken for granted that he could do as much work as two or three other men. Though both these offices were secondary, Cavour became insensibly leader of the house. Questions on whatever subject were answered by him, and he was not careful to consult his chief as to the tenor of his replies. Massimo d' Azeglio said with a rueful smile that he was now like Louis Philippe: he ruled, but did not govern. Cavour stated his own opinions, whether they were popular or unpopular, consonant with those of his party or directly opposed to them. A deputy asked Government to interfere with the mode and substance of the teaching in the seminaries. Cavour immediately answered that he would hold such interference to be a most fatal act of absolutism ; the person to control the instruction given in the seminaries was the bishop ; let bishops play the part of theologians, not of deputies, and let the Government govern, and not play the theologian. Some one pointed out that this was quite at variance with what had been said by the other ministers ; Cavour excused himself towards his colleagues, but repeated that the principle was one of supreme importance. He had spoken "less as a minister than as a politician." And he never learnt to speak otherwise until there was a ministry in which (to borrow a once often quoted witticism) all the ministers were called Cavour.

The energy with which Cavour repudiated the idea of interfering with the seminaries is interesting on other grounds. Possibly he was the only continental statesman who ever saw liberty in an Anglo-Saxon light. This is further shown by the policy he advocated in dealing with the Jesuits. He did not like the Society, which he described as a worse scourge to humanity than communism. You must not judge its real nature, he said, by observing it where its position is contested and precarious. Look at it, rather, where it has a loose rein, where it can apply its rules in a logical and consequent manner, where the whole education of youth is in its hands. The result is *une génération abâtardie*. But the remedy he proposed was not repression. He wished to grant the Jesuits three, four, ten times the liberty they gave to others in the countries under their power. In a free country they could do no harm ; they would be always obliged to modify and transform themselves and would never gain a real empire either in the world of politics or intellect. The great Pombal, who may be called the Cavour of Portugal, took his conception of a free state from England, like the Italian statesman, but he did not understand that persecution is an unfortunate way of inaugurating liberty. This is what for Cavour was "a principle of supreme importance."

In April 1851 Cavour took the office of Minister of Finance ; he had exacted the resignation of his predecessor, Nigra, as the price of his remaining in the Cabinet. The Minister of Public Instruction also resigned owing to disagreements with the now all-powerful member of the Government, and was replaced by a nominee of Cavour's, L. C. Farini, the Romagnol exile, author of *Lo Stato Romano*, whose appointment was significant from a national point of view, notwithstanding his ultra-conservative opinions. Cavour mentioned that Farini's work had been praised by Mr. Gladstone, "one of the most illustrious statesmen in Europe," at which the Chamber applauded wildly, as Cavour intended it to do. Ever watchful for any sign from abroad which could profit Italy, he was glad of what seemed a chance opportunity to provoke a demonstration in honour of the writer of the *Letters to Lord Aberdeen* on the Neapolitan prisons, which were just then creating an immense sensation. In Italy Mr. Gladstone was the most popular man of the hour ; in France, still calling itself a republic, all parties except the reduced ranks of the advanced liberals were very angry—not with King Bomba, but with his accuser. A harmless cousin of Mr. Gladstone

F

was blackballed in a club in Paris on account of the name he bore. Nobody ever had such a good heart as the king of Naples, Count Walewski went about declaring, in support of which he told Mr. Monckton Milnes that Ferdinand had recently granted his request to pardon three hundred prisoners against whom nothing was proved. "How grateful they must have been," replied the Englishman; "did not they come and thank you for having obtained their deliverance?" Taken off his guard and unconscious of the irony, Walewski made the admission that the three hundred were debarred from the pleasure of paying him a visit because, though pardoned, they were not released!

This little story was related to Lord Palmerston, in whom it fanned the fuel of the indignation roused by Mr. Gladstone's *Letters*, of which he had written that "they revealed a system of illegality, injustice, and cruelty which one would not have imagined possible nowadays in Europe." But he employed still stronger language against the Austrians, whose method of reimposing their rule in Lombardy had lost them all their friends in England, for the time at least, and had worked their foes up to the point of fury. Those were the days when they sang at Vienna:

> Hat der Teufel einen Sohn,
> So ist er sicher Palmerston.

Lord Palmerston was coming to a conclusion about Italian matters; it was this: that, great as were the objections to the deliverance of Italy from the Austrians by French aid, yet it would be better for her to be delivered so than not at all. The same conclusion had been reached by Cavour, except that he would not have admitted unending servitude to be the alternative : he was too patriotic and too resourceful for that. He kept in view other contingencies : European complications, the organic disruption of Austria, even at that early date, the foundation of a German empire. But in 1851, as in 1859, the aid of France was the one means of shaking off the Austrian yoke, which was morally certain to succeed. For him, however, the French alliance was only a speck in the distance. He did not think, as Lord Palmerston seems to have thought, that a French liberating army might be " very soon " expected in the Lombard plains. When Louis Napoleon swept away the impediments between himself and the Imperial throne, Cavour was less moved by the violence of the act than by the hope that its consequences might be favourable to Italy. The Prince-President tranquilly awaited the eight million votes which should transform him from a political brigand into a legitimised emperor, and Cavour left him to the judgment of his own countrymen. He saw no need to be more severe than they. It is easy to conceive a higher morality, but as yet it has not been applied to politics. As Cavour remarked, " Franklin sought the help of the most despotic monarch in Europe," and the analogies in recent history do not require to be recalled.

An inferior statesman who, like Cavour, contemplated foreign aid as an ultimate resource, would have lost his interest and slackened his activity in home politics. It was not so with him. Before all other things he placed the necessity of consolidating Piedmont as a constitutional State, and of preparing her morally and materially to take her part in the struggle when it came. If that were not done, a new Bonaparte might indeed cross the Alps in the character of liberator, but a free Italy would be no more the result of his intervention than it had been of his uncle's. Cavour was meditating the stroke of policy which gave him the power to carry out this work of consolidation and preparation. He ruled the ministry, but he did not rule the House and, through it, the country. The Sardinian Chamber of Deputies was composed of the Right Centre, the Extreme Right, the Left Centre, and the Extreme Left. The Extreme Right was loyal to the House of Savoy, but contrary to Italian aspirations; the Extreme Left was strongly Italian, but the degree of its loyalty was hit off in Massimo d'Azeglio's *mot*, "Viva Vittorio, il re provisorio" ("Long live Victor, the provisional king"). There remained the two Centres representing the liberal conservatives and the moderate liberals— "moderate radicals" would be more correct, if the verbal contradiction be permitted. But neither of these single-handed could support a stable and independent government. Every ministry must exist on the sufferance of its opponents, and in terror of the vagaries of the advanced section on its own side. At any critical moment a passing breeze might overthrow it. The only antidote to the recklessness or obstructiveness of extreme parties lay in dissolution; but to dissolve a parliament just elected, as Victor Emmanuel had once been forced to do already, would be a fatal expedient if repeated often.

Any student of representative government would suggest the amalgamation of the two Centres as the true remedy, but so great were the difficulties in the way of this, that not half a dozen persons in Piedmont believed it to be possible. Cavour himself thought about it for a year before making the final move. The acerbities of Italian party politics are not softened by the good social relations and the general mutual confidence in purity of motive which prevail in England. Hitherto Cavour and the brilliant and plausible leader of the Left Centre had not entertained flattering opinions of each other. Rattazzi thought Cavour an ambitious and aggressive publicist rather than a patriot statesman, and Cavour knew Rattazzi to be the minister who led the country to Novara. But he appreciated his value as a parliamentary ally; he had the qualities in which Cavour himself was most deficient. Urbano Rattazzi (born at Alessandria in 1808) was famous as one of the best speakers at the Piedmontese bar before entering the Chamber. He was a perfect master of Italian; his manners were popular and insinuating. He was richly endowed with all those secondary gifts which often carry a man along faster, though less far, than the highest endowments. If he had not power, he had elasticity; if not judgment, cleverness. He always drifted, which made him always appear the politician up to date. His name was then associated with one catastrophe; before he died it was to be linked with two others, Aspromonte and Mentana; but such was his ability as a leader that he retained a compact following to the last.

Cavour rarely made a man's antecedents a reason for not turning him to account; but there was one point on which he required to be reassured before seeking an understanding with Rattazzi — this was whether his

fidelity to the monarchy could be entirely depended on.
Cavour's old friend and fellow worker of the *Risorgimento*,
M. A. Castelli, who was acquainted with the leader of
the Left, opportunely bore witness to Rattazzi's genuine
loyalty, and Cavour hesitated no longer to come to an
agreement which every day proved to be more imperative.   After the *Coup d'état*, the Extreme Right, led by
the Count de Revel and General Menabrea, adopted the
tactics of professing to believe untenable the position of
a free State wedged in between the old despotism of
Austria and the new one of France.   The argument was
ingenious and was likely to make converts.   It was
urgently necessary to form a new political combination
which should reduce this party to impotence.

Cavour's compact with Rattazzi was concluded in the
first month of 1852, but at first it was kept a profound
secret.   It was divulged, as it were, accidentally in the
course of a debate on a Bill which was intended to
moderate the attacks of the press on foreign sovereigns.
This was the only form of restriction which Cavour,
then and afterwards, was willing to countenance.   He
held that the excuse for umbrage given to foreign rulers
by personal invective published in the newspapers was
a danger to the State which no government ought to
tolerate.   The Extreme Right and Left were immediately
up in arms, the first declaring that the Bill did not go far
enough, and the second that it went too far.   Both affected
to consider it the first step to more stringent anti-
liberal measures—invoked by one side and abhorred by
the other.   It was then that Rattazzi made the announcement that although he did not mean to vote for this
particular Bill, he intended to support the Ministry

through the session which had just begun, if, as he
believed, this Bill was an isolated measure, and did not
indicate a change of policy.   Cavour acknowledged the
promise in words which left no doubt that a prior agreement existed between the two leaders.   He repudiated
the reactionary tendencies of Menabrea and his Savoyards, even, he said ironically, at the risk of so great a
misfortune as that of losing the weak support which
they had lately bestowed on Government.   Count de
Revel retorted that the Ministry had divorced the Right
and made a marriage (*connubio*) with the party which
drove Charles Albert to his doom and to an exile's death
in a foreign land.   The alliance between the Centres was
henceforth known by the nickname thus conferred on
it, which has been repeated since by hundreds who have
forgotten its origin.

It is difficult to describe the sensation which this
scene created, and no one was more astonished than
D' Azeglio, who, with the other ministers, had been kept
entirely in the dark.   By all ordinary rules Cavour
ought to have communicated with his colleagues before
revolutionising the parliamentary chessboard.   The more
sure he felt of their opposition the less easy is it to justify
him for taking so grave a step without their knowledge.
On public grounds, however (and these were the only
grounds on which Cavour ever acted in his political life),
it was desirable that the *Connubio* should be an accomplished fact before it was exposed to discussion.
D' Azeglio was very angry, but he hated scandal, and he
refrained from disowning the act of his imperious
colleague.   He was none the less determined never to
sit in the same Cabinet with Rattazzi.   One reason he

gave for it was characteristic. The leader of the Left
had debts, and was not in a hurry to pay them. When
Rattazzi, through Cavour's instrumentality, was elected
President of the Chamber, D'Azeglio felt again aggrieved.
Cavour, who began by treating his chief's antipathy to
his new ally as a prejudice to be made fun of, and in
the end dispelled, came to understand that it was in-
superable. To cut short an impossible situation, he
tendered his resignation, on which all the ministers
resigned ; but as the question was one of personal pique,
the king commanded them to remain at their posts.
Cavour applauded this decision. For the moment it
was better that he, not D'Azeglio, should be sacrificed.
They parted without ceasing to be private and political
friends. Massimo d'Azeglio's nature was too generous
to bear a grudge against the man who was to eclipse
him.

Cavour profited by his reconquered liberty to go to
France and England, a journey that relieved him of the
appearance of wishing to hamper the Cabinet, which
was quickly reconstructed without himself and Farini.
On the eve of starting he went, as etiquette required, to
take leave of the king, who made the not very flattering
remark that he thought it would be a long while before
he called him to power. Cavour must have smiled
behind his spectacles, but he naturally left time to verify
or contradict the royal forecast.

CHAPTER V

THE GREAT MINISTRY

CAVOUR went abroad with the full intention of preparing
for the day when his voice would be that of Piedmont,
if not of Italy. He attached importance to personal
relations, which helped him to keep in touch with
European politics and politicians, and he was anxious to
find out how the *Connubio* was regarded by foreigners,
among whom, till lately, Rattazzi had been looked
upon as a revolutionary firebrand. But thinking men
abroad understood the reasons which had dictated the
coalition. In London Cavour met with a friendly reception from Lord Malmesbury, who was then Foreign
Minister, and who assured him that the English Government would be glad to see him back in office. With
characteristic presence of mind he framed his answer to
provoke a more definite pronouncement. He could not,
he said, return to office alone or abandon the party he
had been at so much pains to create. "Naturally,"
answered Lord Malmesbury, "you cannot return to power
without your friends." Reassured as to the sentiments
of one great political party, Cavour approached the
other in the person of Lord Palmerston, than whom he

never had a firmer political friend or more sincere admirer. Lord Palmerston saw the larger meaning of the experiment of freedom in Piedmont, and he was one of the first to see it. If that experiment succeeded, the Italian tyrannies were doomed ; how, he did not discern, but the fact was apparent to him. He heard, therefore, with much interest what Cavour had to tell him of the gradual taking root of constitutional government in the Sardinian kingdom, and he promised him the moral support, not of one party or another, but of England, "in pledge of which," he added, "we have sent you our best diplomatist." This allusion was to Mr. (afterwards Sir James) Hudson, whom Lord Palmerston had called back from the Brazils in the spring of the year, because by a singular intuition he guessed him to be the very man to help the Italian cause. It was intended to send him to Florence, but when he reached the Foreign Office, which Lord Palmerston had just vacated, he received instructions to go to Turin, a fortunate change of plan. No two men were ever better fitted to work together than Cavour and Sir James Hudson. Without ceasing to be particularly English and strictly loyal to the interests of his own country, the British Minister at Turin served Italy as few of her sons have been able to do. Beneath a rather cold exterior he concealed the warmest of hearts, and he had the power of attaching people to him, so that they never forgot him. It is greatly to be regretted that he left no record of the stirring years of his mission, which coincided with the rise and ascendency of Cavour.

Enchanted with the country, and "more *Anglomane*

than ever," Cavour left England for Paris, where he laid himself out to conciliate political men of all shades, from Morny to Thiers, who advised him to be patient and not to lose heart: "If, after giving you vipers for breakfast, you have another dish served up for dinner, never mind" —such was the diet of politicians. What Cavour once called "his powerful intellectual organisation" made an immediate impression on the Prince President, as he was still styled. Louis Napoleon cultivated an impassible exterior, but at bottom his character was emotional, and, like all emotional persons, he was susceptible to the magnetism of a stronger brain and will. Cavour summoned Rattazzi to Paris to present him to the future Cæsar. "Whether we like it or not," he wrote at this time, "our destinies depend on France; we must be her partner in the great game which will be played sooner or later in Europe." A few weeks later Napoleon declared at Bordeaux that "the empire was peace," but like all intelligent onlookers Cavour received the statement with incredulity. Possibly the only person who believed in it was the speaker—for the moment; he may have thought that "bread and games" was a formula by which he could rule France, or rather Paris, but he was soon to find it insufficient.

Cavour sought out several of the Italian exiles who were leading a life of privation and obscurity in Paris, one of whom was Manin, the Dictator of Venice. With him Cavour expressed himself "very much satisfied, though his sentiments were rather too Venetian": sentiments which Manin sacrificed—a last act of abnegation —when he finally gave his support to Italian unity under Victor Emmanuel, carrying with him two-thirds of the

republican party, who could brave the charge of changed
allegiance if so incorruptible a patriot led the way.
Cavour also saw Gioberti, "always the same child of
genius, who would have been a great man had he had
common sense." Gioberti, however, had made a great
stride towards common sense, for instead of dreaming
of liberating popes, he was now imagining a renovating
statesman, and he had inscribed Cavour's name under
his new portrait. In a book published in Paris, Gioberti
drew the Cavour of the future with a penetration and a
sureness of touch which would make a reader, who did
not know the date, suppose that the words were written
ten years later. Men of great talent, he said, rarely
threw aside the chance of becoming famous; rather did
they snatch it with avidity; and what fame more splendid
could now be won than that of the minister of the Italian
prince who should re-make the country? He fixed his
hopes on Cavour, because he alone understood that in
human society civilisation is everything, all the rest,
without it, nothing. "He knows that statutes, parliaments, newspapers, all the appurtenances of free governments, even if they are of use to individuals, are miserable
shams to the commonalty if they fail to help forward
social progress." He was willing to forgive him the
generous error of treating a province as if it were a
nation, when he compared it with the pettiness of those
who treated the nation as if it were a province. He
invoked some great and solemn act of *Italianità* on
his part, which should pledge him irrevocably to the
national cause. Cavour was too little influenced by
others for it to be safe to say that this was one of the
prophecies which tend to their own fulfilment; still

it is worth noticing that he read the passage and was struck by it.

Cavour had scarcely returned to Piedmont when a ministerial crisis occurred through the rejection by the Senate of a far from stringent Bill for permitting civil marriage, which had passed in the Chamber of Deputies. The situation was further complicated by the state of mind into which the king had been driven by the remonstrances of his wife and mother, both near their end, and by the answer which he received from Rome in reply to a direct appeal to settle matters amicably, the Pope having said, in effect, that he was not going to help him to legalise concubinage in his dominions. D'Azeglio, harassed on all sides and ill through the reopening of his wound, resigned office, and advised the king to send for Cavour. "The other one, whom you know, is diabolically active, and fit in body and soul, and then, he enjoys it so much!" he wrote to a friend, with the pathetic wonder of the artist, romancist, and *grand seigneur*, who had never been able to make out what there was to enjoy in politics. Victor Emmanuel followed his advice, but he allowed Cavour to see that he hoped that the new ministry would make up the quarrel with Rome. Cavour knew that only one path could lead to peace — surrender. Though anxious for office he declined to take it on these terms, and he recommended the king to call Count Balbo to his counsels ; but Balbo, persuaded that a ministry only supported by the Extreme Right could not stand even for a few weeks, in his turn suggested the recall of D'Azeglio. Here the saving good sense of the king interposed ; little as he liked Cavour he recognised that he was the only man possible, and he charged him, without conditions, with the formation of a ministry. D' Azeglio had fallen on a point on which Cavour was for and not against him; his successor desired to show that there would be no violent change of policy, and he therefore reconstructed the Cabinet as it was before, except for the change of head. He reserved for himself the Presidency of the Council and the Ministry of Finance. Rattazzi, who still occupied the Speaker's chair, was willing to wait for the present for a seat in the Cabinet, especially when he heard that the king, who was at first very hostile to the *Connubio*, had quite expected him to take office.

So the *gran ministero*, as it was called, entered upon its functions : great by reason of its chief, who infused his own life and vigour into what was before a weak administration. Cavour was a born man of business; he hated disorder in everything—except, indeed, dress, in which his carelessness was proverbial. He had not the common belief that, muddle them how you may, there will always be a providence which looks after the affairs of the State and prevents the collapse that would attend a private commercial enterprise conducted on the same system. He took in hand the financial renewal of Piedmont in the same spirit in which, when he had only just reached maturity, he volunteered to restore his father's dilapidated fortune. It was for this that he chose the Ministry of Finance : Piedmont, as he saw, could never sustain a national and Italian policy abroad without having first set its own house in order. He started with two principles : taxation must be increased and the resources of the country must be so developed as to enable it to pay its way without sinking into hopeless stagnation. It was a disappointment to some to see Cavour devoting himself with more ardour to putting on new taxes than to producing any of those decorative schemes for hastening the millennium which are expected from a new and ambitious minister. But, though ambitious, he cared for the substance, power—not for the shadow, popularity.

If there had been no other reason for the compact with the moderate liberals, the necessity for fresh taxation would have been a sufficing one. The Extreme Right and Left proposed to meet the existing difficulties by cutting down expenditure, but, if sound in theory, in practice this policy would have reduced Piedmont to complete impotence. While a part of the Left Centre voted with the extremists, it was only by the greatest efforts that a grant of £100,000 was obtained for the fortifications of Casale, which had been declared by the war minister, La Marmora, to be absolutely necessary for the defence of the State. The radical deputy Brofferio said that States wanted no other defence than the breasts of their citizens. From the Chamber, as then constituted, there was little hope of obtaining the imposition of new burdens, in part designed to meet Sardinian liabilities, but in part also to render possible the reorganisation of the army, which was urgently required if the future was not to witness disasters worse than those already experienced. Prince Metternich had said that, even if Piedmont were so troublesome as to persist in her liberal infatuation, she would have to keep quiet, at a moderate computation, for twenty years—just the time which it took her king to unite Italy. The two campaigns of 1848-1849 and the war indemnity

had cost about 300,000,000 frs. The annual expenditure
was doubled. Added to this, the one source of wealth,
agriculture, was almost ruined by the oidium disease
which destroyed the vines, and by harvests so bad that
the like had not been seen since the celebrated scarcity
which followed the wars of Napoleon. As Cavour saved
his father's property not by burying the last talent in a
safe place but by laying it out in bold improvements, so
now he did not fear to spend largely and even lavishly,
not only on the army, but also on public works. He
completed the railway system and employed what
Brofferio called "a portentous activity" in extending
the roads, canals, and all the means of communication
which could stimulate industry. It must be remembered
that Piedmont was then lamentably backward; a long
obscurantist *régime*, succeeded by war and havoc, had left
her destitute of all the accessories of modern life. This
was changed as if by the wand of the magician. In his
first budget, Cavour put on new taxes to the amount of
14,000,000 frs., one being the so-called tax on patents,
or on the exercise of trades and professions, which excited
much adverse criticism. At the same time he reduced
the salt tax and initiated several free-trade measures, to
be ultimately crowned by the abolition of the corn laws.
On the whole, however, his line of policy was not such
as would recommend itself to the crowd, and in October
1853 a furious mob attacked the Palazzo Cavour, repeating the old cry that the minister was a monopolist who
robbed the poor of their bread. Luckily the doors were
barred, but next day Cavour was threatened as he
walked along the streets. Just then the Ministry of
Justice fell vacant, and it was offered to Rattazzi, who,

to his credit be it said, did not hesitate to take office
at a time when the head of the Government was the
target of unscrupulous abuse, and it was even thought
that his life was in danger. Rattazzi was afterwards
transferred to the Home Ministry, which he held till the
Connubio broke up, more on personal than on political
grounds, in 1858.

Though Cavour's alliance with Rattazzi was not
eternal, it lasted till it had served its purpose. By help
of it he imposed his will on king and country until he
was strong enough to impose it by force of his own com-
manding influence. He always considered the *Connubio*
one of the wisest acts of his political life. It is not
uncommon to hear it still denounced in Italy as the
origin of the political demoralisation, the mixing up of
private and public interests, the lack of fixed principles;
which later times have witnessed. If the fact were
admitted, it would not show that Cavour could have
governed in any other way. Had the country trusted
him from the first it would have been different, but the
country did not trust him. Even after the combination
of the two Centres, whenever there was a general election
it was doubtful if the Government would obtain a working majority. The accusation of corruption was frequently made against the Ministry in general and
Rattazzi in particular, since it was he who presided over
the electoral campaigns. Of corruption in the literal
sense there was probably little, but constituencies were
led to believe that it would be to their advantage to
return the ministerial candidate. On one occasion
Rattazzi tried to prove that such hints did not constitute
" interference." Cavour got up in the course of the

same debate and not only acknowledged the "interference," but said that without it constitutional government in Piedmont would collapse. His biographers have preferred to be silent on this subject, but he would have despised a reserve which conceals historical facts. The apathy of one section of the electors, the fads and jealousies of another, the feverish longing to pull down whomsoever was in power, inherited from a great revolutionary crisis, the indefatigable propaganda of clerical wire-pullers, all tended to the formation of parliaments so composed as to bring government to a standstill. The result of a protracted interruption might be the fall of the constitution itself, or it might be civil war. Cavour took the means open to him to prevent it, and, whether he was right or wrong, his career cannot be judged if the difficulties with which he had to cope are kept out of sight.

Piedmont needed some years, not of rest, but of active and consecutive labour before it could enter the lists again as armed champion of Italian independence. The disastrous issue of the last conflicts had been attributed to every cause except that which was most accountable for it : a badly led and badly organised army. The "We are betrayed" theory was caught up alike by republicans and conservatives, who accused each other of ruining the country rather than give the victory to the rival faction. Whatever grain of truth there was in these taunts, the military inefficiency of the forces which Charles Albert led across the Ticino in March 1848 remained the main reason why Radetsky was able to get back Lombardy and Venetia for his master. This Cavour knew, and he was anxious not to precipitate matters till La

Marmora, to whom he privately gave *carte blanche*, could
say that his work was done. He began treating Austria
with more consideration than she had received from
Massimo d' Azeglio, who was a bad hand at dissembling.
Count Buol was gratified, almost grateful. But these
relatively harmonious relations did not last long. In
February 1853 there was an abortive attempt at revolution in Milan, of which not one person in a thousand
knew anything till it was suppressed. It was the
premature and ill-advised explosion of a conspiracy by
which Mazzini hoped to repeat the miracle of 1848 : the
ejection of a strong military power by a blast of popular
fury. But miracles are not made to order, though
Mazzini never came to believe it. As a reprisal for this
disturbance, the Austrian Government, not content with
executions and bastinadoes, decreed the sequestration of
the lands of those Lombard emigrants who had become
naturalised in Piedmont. Cavour charged Austria with
a breach of international law and recalled the Sardinian
minister from Vienna. It was risking war, but he knew
that even for the weakest state there are some things
worse than war. It was reversing the policy of prudence
with which he had set out, but when prudence meant
cowardice, Cavour always cast it to the winds. The
outcry in all Europe against the sequestration decree
deterred the Austrian Government from treating the
Sardinian protest as a *casus belli*. Liberal public
opinion everywhere approved of Cavour's course, and in
France and England increased confidence was felt in
him by those in authority. Governments like to deal
with a strong man who knows when not to fear.

Only such a man would have conceived the idea

which was now taking concrete form in Cavour's mind. This was the plan of an armed alliance with the Western Powers on the outbreak of the war, which as early as November 1853 well-informed persons looked upon as henceforth inevitable. Cavour would never have been a Chauvinist, but he was not by nature a believer in neutrality. He was constitutionally inclined to think that in all serious contingencies to act is safer than not to act. The world is divided between men of this mould and their opposites. La Marmora told him that the army, which had made incredible progress considering the state in which it was a short time before, could place in the field a force for which no country would have reason to blush. If not a great general, the Piedmontese Minister of War might fairly be called a first-class organiser. For the rest, Cavour believed that the ultimate school of any army is war. Above all, he believed that this was the hour for a great resolve or a *gran rifiuto*. If the House of Savoy stood still with folded arms it might retire into the ranks of small ruling families, which leave the rearrangement of maps to their betters. It was secretly reported to Cavour that Napoleon III. was beginning to drop enigmatical remarks about Italian affairs, and it was these reports that finally decided him to strain every nerve to make his audacious design a reality.

Russia had broken off diplomatic relations with Sardinia in 1848, and when Victor Emmanuel communicated the death of his father to the Powers, the only one which returned no response was the empire of the Czar. It would be absurd to adduce this lack of courtesy as an excuse for war; still it gave a slightly better complexion to an attack which the Russian Government was justified in calling "extraordinarily gratuitous." Cavour had one person of great importance on his side, the king. In January 1854 he broached the subject with the tentative inquiry, "Does it not seem to your Majesty that we might find some way of taking part in the war of the Western Powers with Russia?" To which Victor Emmanuel answered simply, "If I cannot go myself I will send my brother." But it is not too much to say that the whole country was against him. The old Savoyard party opposed the war tooth and nail, and from the "Little Piedmont" point of view it was perfectly right. The radicals, headed by Brofferio, denounced it as "economically reckless, militarily a folly, politically a crime." Most of the Lombard emigration thought ill of it, and the heads of the army were lukewarm or contrary; this was not the war they wanted. The Tuscan romancist Guerrazzi wrote, with unpardonable levity, that republicans ought to rejoice because this was the final disillusion given to Italians by monarchy, limited or not. One republican, however, Manin, saw in the Italian tricolor displayed with the French and English flags in Paris the first ray of hope that had gladdened his eyes since he left Venice, and Poerio, when he heard of the alliance in his dungeon, "felt his chain grow lighter." It seemed as if those who had suffered most for Italy had a clearness of vision denied to the rest.

What, if persisted in, would have been the most serious obstacle was the opposition of Rattazzi, but he was won over to assent, if not to approval, by Giuseppe Lanza, a new figure on the parliamentary scene, who had lately been elected Vice-President of the Chamber. Lanza (who was destined to be Prime Minister when the Italians went to Rome) was then only slightly acquainted with Cavour; from being independent, his favourable opinion carried more weight. With Rattazzi's adhesion the majority of the Centres was secured. It was not an enthusiastic majority, but it quieted its forebodings by the argument which was beginning to take hold of people's minds: that Cavour must be let do as he chose. Hardly any one liked him, but to see him stand there, absolutely unhesitating and sure, among the politicians of Buts and Ifs, began to generate the belief that he was a man of fate who must be allowed to go his way.

It is easy to be wise after the event, and it may seem strange now that the alliance with the Western Powers found so few, so very few cordial supporters. But Cavour himself called the risks which attended it "enormous." The great question for Sardinia was what Austria would do. If she did nothing, the pros and cons were perhaps evenly balanced; if she joined Russia, the pros would be strengthened; if she joined the allies, the situation for Sardinia would be grave indeed. The republicans were already calling the war an alliance with Austria. Were the description verified, it was hard to see how the utmost genius or skill could draw aught but evil from so unnatural a union.

The first invitation to Sardinia to co-operate came separately from England, which had vetoed a monstrous proposal on the part of Austria to occupy Alessandria, in order, in any case, to prevent Piedmont from attacking her during the war. Lord Clarendon instructed Sir

James Hudson to represent to Cavour that Austria's
fears would be set at rest if a portion of the Sardinian
army were sent to the East. The chief English motive
was really the conviction that numbers were urgently
required if the war was to succeed, and also the desire
to lessen the large numerical superiority of the French.
In the first instance Cavour replied that although he had
been all along in favour of participating in the war, his
Cabinet was too much against the idea for him to take
any immediate action. But the subject was revived. An
alliance with Piedmont was popular in England, where the
Government was in an Italian mood, having been made
terribly angry by the King of Naples' prohibition of the
sale of mules for transport purposes in the East. In
December 1854 Cavour was formally invited to send a
corps which would enter the English service and receive
its pay from the British Exchequer. He would rather
have sent it on these terms than not at all, but the
scheme met with such unqualified condemnation from
La Marmora and General Dadormida, the Foreign
Minister, that it was set aside as not becoming to the
dignity of an independent nation. Meanwhile something had occurred which reinforced the arguments of
those who were against sending troops at all. After
hedging for a year, Austria signed a treaty couched in
vague terms, but which appeared to debar her, at any
rate, from taking sides with Russia—Italy's most flattering prospect. Napoleon III. expected much more from
it than this; he thought that Austria was too much
compromised to avoid throwing in her cause with the
allies. It must be said of Napoleon that among the
men responsible for the Crimean War he alone aimed at

an object which, from a political, let alone moral view, could justify it. He did not think that it would be enough to obtain a few restrictions, not worth the paper on which they were written, and the prospect of a new lease of life to Turkish despotism. He certainly had one paltry object of his own ; he wished to gratify his subjects by military glory. He began to suspect the hollowness of the testimony of the plebiscite ; the French people did not like him, and never would like him. A war would please the populace and the army ; it would also make him look much more like a real Napoleon. But when he had decided to go to war, he hoped to do something worth doing. He thought (to use his own words) "that no peace would be satisfactory which did not resuscitate Poland." There, and nowhere else, were the wings of the Russian eagle to be clipped. Moreover, the entire French nation, which cared so little for Italy, would have applauded the deliverance of Poland. On the Polish question the ultramontane would have embraced the socialist. France was never so united as in the sympathy which she then felt for Poland, except in that which she now feels for Russia. But Napoleon did not think that he could resuscitate Poland without Austrian assistance. At the close of 1854 he made sure of getting it.

Cavour clung to his project. Probably his penetrating mind guessed that Austria could not fight Russia, which had saved her from destruction in 1849. There now arose a demand for some guarantee which should give Piedmont, if she took part in the war, at least the certainty of a moral advantage. The king remarked to the French Ambassador that all this wrangling about

conditions was folly : "If we ally ourselves promptly
and frankly, we shall gain a great deal more." Doubtless Cavour thought the same, but to satisfy the country
it was necessary to demand, if nothing else, a promise
from the Western Powers that they would put pressure
on Austria to raise the sequestrations on the property of
the Lombard exiles. But the Powers, which were court-
ing Austria, refused to make any such promise, on which
the Foreign Minister, General Dadormida, resigned,
notwithstanding that the Lombard emigrants generously
begged the Government not to think of them. Cavour
offered the Foreign Office and the Presidency of the
Council to D'Azeglio, under whom he would have consented to serve, but D'Azeglio declined to enter the
Ministry, whilst engaging not to oppose its policy.
Cavour then took the Foreign Office himself, and at
eight o'clock on the evening of the same day, January 10,
1855, the protocol of the offensive and defensive alliance
of Sardinia with France and England was, at last,
signed.

Writing of the Crimean War in after days, Louis
Kossuth observed that never did a statesman throw
down a more hazardous and daring stake than Cavour
when he insisted on clenching the alliance after he had
found out that it must be done without any conditions
or guarantees. Cicero's *Partem fortuna sibi vindicat*
applies to diplomacy as well as to war, "but the stroke
was very bold and very dangerous."

CHAPTER VI

THE speeches made by Cavour in defence of the alliance before the two Houses of Parliament contain the clearest exposition of his political faith that he had yet given. They form a striking refutation of the theory, still held by many, especially in Italy, that he was lifted into the sphere of high political aims by a whirlwind none of his sowing. In these speeches he is less occupied with Piedmont, the kingdom of which he was Prime Minister, than an English statesman who required war supplies would be with Lancashire. "I shall be asked," he said, "how can this treaty be of use to Italy?" The treaty would help Italy in the only way in which, in the actual conditions of Europe, she could be helped. The experience of the last years and of the past centuries had shown that plots and revolutions could not make Italy; "at least," he added, "in my opinion it has shown it." What, then, could make her? The raising of her credit. To raise Italy's credit two things were needed: the proof that an Italian Government could combine order with liberty, and the proof that Italians could fight. He was certain that the laurels won by Sardinian soldiers in the

East would do more for Italy than all that had been done by those who thought to effect her regeneration by rhetoric.

When Cavour spoke of himself in public, it was generally in a light tone, and half in jest. Thus in the debate on the treaty, he said that Brofferio and his friends could not be surprised at his welcoming the English alliance when they had once done nothing but tax him with Anglomania, and had given him the nickname of Milord Risorgimento. He could easily have aroused enthusiasm if, instead of this banter, he had spoken the words of passionate earnestness in which he alluded to his part in the transaction in a letter to Mme. de Circourt. He felt, he said, the tremendous responsibility which weighed on him, and the dangers which might arise from the course adopted, but duty and honour dictated it. Since it had pleased Providence that Piedmont, alone in Italy, should be free and independent, Piedmont was bound to make use of its freedom and independence to plead before Europe the cause of the unhappy peninsula. This perilous task the king and the country were resolved to persevere in to the end. Those French liberals and doctrinaires who were now weeping over the loss of liberty in France, after helping to stifle it in Italy, might consider his policy absurd and romantic; he exposed himself to their censures, sure that all generous hearts would sympathise with the attempt to call back to life a nation which for centuries had been shut up in a horrible tomb. If he failed, he reckoned on his friend reserving him a place among the "eminent vanquished" who gathered round her; in any case she would take the vent he had given to his feelings as the avowal *that all his life was conse-crated to one sole work, the emancipation of his country.* This was not a boast uttered to bring down the plaudits of the Senate; it was a confession which escaped from Cavour in one of the rare moments when, even in private, he allowed himself to say what he felt. But it speaks to posterity with a voice which silences calumny.

After the point had been gained and the war em-barked upon, the anxieties of the minister who was solely responsible for it did not decrease. The House of Savoy had survived Novara ; one royal sacrifice served the purpose of an ancient immolation ; it pro-pitiated fate. But a Novara in the East would have been serious indeed. What Cavour feared, however, was not defeat—it was inaction, of which the moral effect would have been nearly as bad. What if the laurels he had spoken of were never won at all ? The position of the Sardinian contingent on the first line was not secured without endless diplomacy ; Napoleon wished to keep it out of sight as a reserve corps at Con-stantinople. When, with the aid of England, it was shipped for Balaclava, there still seemed a disposition to hold it back. Cavour wrote bitterly of the prospect of the Sardinian troops being sent by the allies to perish of disease in the trenches while they advanced at the pace of a yard a month. He described himself and his colleagues as waiting with cruel impatience for tidings of the first engagement : "Still no news from the army ; it is distracting !" Meanwhile the "Reds" and the "Blacks" were happy. Cavour did not fear the first, except, perhaps, at Genoa ; but he did fear

the deeply-rooted forces of reaction, which were only
too likely to regain the ascendant if things went wrong
with the war.

At last the long-desired, almost despaired-of news
arrived. On August 16 the Piedmontese fought an
engagement on the Tchernaia; it was not a great battle,
but it was a success, and the men showed courage and
steadiness. It was hailed at Turin as a veritable god-
send. The king, jaded and worn out by the trials which
this year had brought him, rejoiced as sovereign and
soldier at the prowess of his young troops. The public
underwent a general conversion to the war policy; every
one thought in secret he had always approved of it.
The little flash of glory called attention to the other
merits of the Piedmontese soldier besides those he
displayed in the field. These merits were truly great.
The troops bore with the utmost patience the terrible
scourge of the cholera, which cost them 1200 lives.
Their English allies were never tired of admiring the
good organisation and neatness of their camp, which
was laid out in huts that kept off the burning sun better
than tents, intersected with paths and gardens. The
little army was fortified by the feeling that after all it
was serving no alien cause but its own. "Never mind,"
said a soldier, as they were struggling in the slough of
the trenches, "of this mud Italy will be made." They
all shared the hope which the king expressed in a letter
to La Marmora, "Next year we shall have war where
we had it before."

Victor Emmanuel's visit to the courts of Paris and
London was not without political significance. Cavour
first intended that only D'Azeglio should accompany

him; he always put the Marquis forward when he wished the country to appear highly respectable and anti-revolutionary; at the last moment he decided to go himself as well. In Paris the king was dismayed at observing that Napoleon, in presence of Austria's in-action, was bent on making peace. Cavour had also counted on the continuance of the war, but he found encouragement in the fact that when he left, the Emperor told him to write confidentially to Walewski what, in his opinion, he could do for Piedmont and Italy. In England the king was most cordially received, and, if he was rather embarrassed when a portion of the English religious world hailed him as a kind of new Luther, he could not help being struck by the real friendliness shown to him by all classes. Cavour made a strongly favourable impression on Prince Albert, and the Queen expressed so much sympathy with his aims that he called her "the best friend of Piedmont in England." He carried away a curious souvenir of his visit to Windsor. When Victor Emmanuel was made Knight of the Garter, the Queen wished that he should know the meaning of the oath he took; whereupon Lord Palmerston at once wrote down a translation of the words into Italian, and handed it to the king. When Cavour heard of this, he asked the king to give him the paper to preserve in the Sardinian archives.

The preliminaries of the peace were signed in February 1856. It was a great blow to Victor Emmanuel, who had felt confident that if the war lasted long enough for Russia to be placed in real danger, Austria would be obliged to go to her assistance. The heavy bill for war expenditure, largely exceeding the estimate, damped

people's spirits, buoyed up for an instant by victory,
and they asked once more, what was the good of it all?
Time was to answer the question; but before showing
how an issue, which even Cavour viewed with disappointment, proved, nevertheless, fruitful of more good
than the most sanguine advocate of the war had ven-
tured to hope for, a short account must be given of the
home politics of Piedmont in the year 1855.

"Battles long ago" never wholly lose their interest.
The mere words, "There was once a battle fought here"
make the traveller stop and think, even if he does not
know by what men of what race it was fought. But
the parliamentary struggles of one generation seem
passing stale and unprofitable to the next. Yet the
history of nations depends as much on their civil as on
their warlike contests. In Piedmont the strife always
turned on the same point: whether the State or the
Church should predominate. Free institutions do not
settle the question; it is most manifestly rife to-day in
a free country, Canada. In Italy itself a great clerical
party is working silently but ceaselessly, under the mask
of abstention from the elections, to recover its political
power. The Sardinian Government could not withdraw
from the duel at will; the Church in Piedmont was a
political force constantly on the lookout for an opening
to retake the position it had lost. Besides the moral
power derived from the support of the peasants and of
the old aristocracy, it wielded the material power of
an organised body, which was numerous and wealthy
in proportion to the numbers and wealth of the
population. The annual income of the Church, including the religious houses, was nearly £700,000 a

year. There were 23,000 ecclesiastics, or 1 monk to every 670 inhabitants, 1 nun to every 1695, 1 priest to every 214. In spite of the vast resources of the Church, the parish priest in 2540 villages received a stipend of less than £20 per year. Not only radicals but many moderate politicians were of opinion that the great number of convents of the contemplative orders formed an actual evil from the fact of their encouraging able-bodied idleness, and the withdrawal of so considerable a fraction of the population from the work and duties of citizenship. In the autumn of 1854, before the Crimean War was thought of, Rattazzi framed a bill by which the corporations that took no part in public instruction, preaching, or nursing the sick, were abolished. Since the last crisis on the civil marriage bill, which wrecked D'Azeglio's ministry, Cavour, who all his life was not theoretically opposed to coming to an understanding with Rome, had made several advances to the Vatican, but with no effect: Rome refused any modification of the Concordat or any reduction of the privileges possessed by the clergy in the kingdom of Sardinia. On the failure of these negotiations, Victor Emmanuel despatched three high ecclesiastics on a private mission to the Pope to see if the quarrel could be made up. This mission, which might have seriously compromised the king, was not counselled by Cavour, who put a violent end to it when he authorised Rattazzi to bring in the bill for the suppression of religious houses. Victor Emmanuel was deeply mortified, and the Pope protested against this new "horrible and incredible assault of the subalpine Government." Just at the time that the measure was discussed in Parliament, the king lost his mother, his wife, his infant child, and his brother, a series of misfortunes in which the Church saw " the finger of God." As the two queens and the Duke of Genoa were devoted Catholics, their last hours were rendered miserable by the impending sacrilegious act. It is not to be wondered if the king was almost driven out of his mind.

After the lugubrious interruption of the royal funerals, the debate on the religious corporations was resumed with new vigour. Much the most effective speeches on either side were those delivered by the combatants of the two extremes, Brofferio and Count Solaro de la Margherita. Brofferio, who regarded all convents as a specific evil, had proposed their indiscriminate abolition in 1848, directly after the promulgation of the Statute. Cavour, he said, had then defended them. Was he therefore, mindful of their old warfare, to vote against this Bill in order to place difficulties in the way of the Ministry ? Far from it. If the Government were willing to abolish all the convents, so much the better; if 490, he would vote for that; if 245, he was ready to approve; if 100, yes ; if 10, he would vote for 10 ; if one convent, he agreed ; if one monk, his vote would be given for the abolition of one monk. He would not imitate those speakers who had attempted to conjure up a canonical or theological defence of the Bill. The Pope was probably a better theologian than he ; but he denied that the Church had any prescriptive rights at all : all her privileges and property being held on sufferance of the State, which could withdraw its toleration when it chose. Illustrious Italians, from Dante downwards, denounced the love of

H

power and money of the Church as the bane of Italy.
Had not Machiavelli said, " If Italy has fallen a prey
not only to powerful barbarians but to whatsoever
attack, we Italians are indebted for it to the Church
and to nothing else " ? Respect for the intentions of the
pious founder was a good thing in its way (Brofferio
had the sense to see that this was the strongest argument
of the opposite party), yet, logically pursued, it would
have obliged us to this day to preserve the temple of
Delphi with a full chapter of priests. Some one might
have got up and said, " A very interesting result " ; but
Neo-Hellenism did not grow in the Sardinian Chamber
of Deputies. Brofferio censured the exemption of the
teaching and preaching orders—according to him, the
most mischievous of all. He blamed the Ministry for
excusing the measure on financial grounds. Either it
was just or it was unjust. If just, it needed no excuse ;
if unjust, no excuse could justify it. There was, he said,
no use in trying to make the Bill appear moderate in
the hopes that it would be borne more patiently by the
body against which it was aimed. The Court of Rome
knew no more or less. War to the knife or refusal to
kiss the Pope's toe : it was all one.

As the stoutest champion of the Bill was the Béranger
of Piedmont, with his rough and ready eloquence, so its
most formidable critic was the old apostle of thrones
and altars, who would have taken Philip II. as a model
king, and Torquemada as an ideal statesman. His
onslaught was far stronger than the strictures of less
out-and-out reactionaries. It was easy, for instance, to
accuse of weakness the amiable sentimentality of the
Marquis Gustavo Cavour, who evoked Padre Cristoforo

from Manzoni's *Promessi Sposi* to plead for his fellow
friars ; but there was no destroying the force, so far as
it went, of Count Solaro's question, Were they Catholics,
or were they not ? To endorse a policy not approved by
the Church was to cease, *ipso facto*, to be a Catholic.
The reasoning might not be true, but it was clear.
Charles Albert's old minister drew a beautiful picture
of the country in the good old times before the Statute.
Then the people did not lack bread. Life and property
and the good name of citizens were safeguarded. The
finances were not exhausted ; the taxes were not exces-
sive ; the revenue was not diminishing ; treaties were
observed ; Piedmont possessed that consideration of
foreign courts which a wise government can always
command, even without the prestige of force :—a picture
drawn in a fine artistic free-hand, not slavishly subser-
vient to fact ; but as to the taxes, at least, its correctness
was not to be gainsaid. Seen from this point of view,
the progress of all modern States means retrogression,
a paradox which has passed now from the friends of the
old order, few of whom have still the courage to sustain it, to the socialists, the sum of whose contentions
it exactly formulates. Count Solaro enlarged on the
dreadful evils that would result from the Bill were it to
become law, not to the religious corporations, which
a wiser generation and renewed endowments would
restore to more than their pristine prosperity, but to
the country which suffered the perpetration of a sin so
enormous that words were powerless to describe it.

After the war dances of Brofferio and Solaro de la
Margherita, Cavour made a temperate speech, in which
he said that he agreed with Brofferio in placing moral

expediency above a question of finance, but that if this were granted, the Government could not be indifferent, in the present state of the finances, to a saving of nearly a million francs a year (it being proposed to defray out of the confiscated ecclesiastical property a grant to that amount which the State paid to the poorer clergy). He defended the expropriation of a convent called Santa Croce to meet the need of a hospital for the military cholera patients. Passing on to larger considerations, he recognised the great services rendered by religious orders in past times, when Europe was emerging from barbarism, and was still a prey to the violence and ignorance of feudal society. Had the religious communities not met a want, they would not have taken root. Civilisation, literature, agriculture, and above all the poor, neglected and oppressed by the secular power, owed them an immense debt. But coming down to the present day, Cavour argued that the original part played by monks and friars was now filled, and of necessity more efficaciously filled, by laymen. Their presence in superabundant numbers in the modern State was an anachronism. It was only needful to compare the countries where they abounded in number and in influence, as in Spain and the kingdom of Naples, with England, Prussia, or France, to see whether it was possible to allege that they tended to enlightenment and prosperity.

The Bill was passed in the Chamber of Deputies on March 2, 1855, by 170 ayes against 36 noes; the majority, so much larger than the Government could usually command, showed that it rested on undoubted popular support. It was then sent up to the Senate, but

while it was being discussed there, an incident occurred
which nearly caused a political convulsion. The Archbishop of Novara and the Bishop of Mondovì wrote to
the king promising that if the Bill were withdrawn,
the Church in Piedmont would make up the sum of
92,841,230 frs., which the Government expected to gain
by the suppressions. The king was delighted with the
proposal, not perceiving the hopelessness of getting it
approved by the Chamber of Deputies, which had
already passed the measure, and the impossibility of
settling the matter "out of court" without parliamentary
sanction. He invited Cavour to accede, and on his
refusal, he accepted the resignation of the Ministry.
Personally the king had always a certain sense of relief
in parting with Cavour. He thought now that he could
get on without him, but he was to be undeceived.
While he was endeavouring to find some one to undertake the formation of a new cabinet, the country became
agitated as it had not been since the stormy year of
revolution. Angry crowds gathered in Piazza Castello,
within a few yards of the royal palace. "One of these
days," Victor Emmanuel said impatiently to his trusted
valet, Cinzano, "I'll make an end of these demonstrations,"
to which the descendant of Gil Blas is reported to have
replied as he looked out of window: "And if they made
an end of Us?" The whole population woke up to the
fact that surrender on this point involved surrender
along all the line. The king, however, to whom the
compromise appeared in the light of peace with the dead
and with the living, with the Superga and with the
Vatican, was very unwilling to yield. At the same
time no one could be found to form a ministry. In this

dangerous crisis, Massimo d' Azeglio wrote a letter to his
sovereign which is believed to have been what convinced
him.   Recalling the Spanish royal personage whom
courtiers let burn to death sooner than deviate from the
motto, *ne touchez pas la Reine,* D' Azeglio protested that if
he was to risk his head, or totally to lose the king's
favour, he would think himself the vilest of mankind if
he did not write the words which he had not been permitted to speak.   As an old and faithful servant, who
had never thought but of his king's welfare and the
good of the country, he conjured him with tears in his
eyes, and kneeling at his feet, to go no further on the
path he was entering.   A monkish intrigue had succeeded in breaking up the work of his reign, agitating
the country, shaking the constitution and obscuring the
royal name for good faith.   There was not a moment to
lose; similar intrigues had led the House of Bourbon
and the House of Stuart to their destruction.   Let the
king take heed while there was time!   It was long
before Victor Emmanuel quite forgave his old friend,
but the warning voice was not raised in vain.

Cavour was recalled.   The Bill was presented again
to the Senate with some slight modifications.   One
religious order was spared by Rattazzi, rather against
the will of Cavour, who described it as "absolutely
useless," because the king particularly wished to save it,
the nuns having been favourites of his mother.   To
Cavour, Victor Emmanuel's resistance had seemed simply
a fit of superstitious folly; he did not sufficiently realise
how distasteful the whole affair must be to a man like
the king, who said to General Durando when he was
starting for the Crimea, "You are fortunate, General, in

going to fight the Russians, while I stay here to fight monks and nuns." In its amended form the Bill passed on May 29. Cavour had triumphed completely, but he came out of the struggle physically and mentally exhausted ; "a struggle," he wrote to his Geneva friends, "carried on in Parliament, in the drawing-rooms, at the court as in the street, and rendered more painful by a crowd of distressing events." As usual he sought refreshment in the fields of Leri, and when, after a brief rest, he returned to Turin, the furious passions which had surged round this domestic duel were beginning to cool as the eyes of the nation became more and more fixed on the conflict in the East and its significance to Italy.

We can proceed now with the story of Cavour's work in the memorable year which opened so gloomily with a truce that appeared to leave *felix Austria* mistress of the situation. Without firing a shot, that Power could consider herself the chief gainer by the war. Napoleon III., anxious for peace, welcomed her mediation, and in England, though peace was unpopular, and Austrian selfishness during the war had not been admired, Lord Palmerston was handicapped by the idea which just then occupied his mind, that Austria chiefly stood in the way of what, as an Englishman, he most feared in European politics, a Franco-Russian alliance. He divined the probability, almost the inevitability, of such an alliance at a date when most persons would have thought it an absurd fiction. Thus, in January 1856, both the French and English Governments were in a phase of opinion which promised nothing to Italian aspirations. The question was, Would it be possible for one capable brain

to bend them to its purposes? In the first instance,
Cavour believed that it would not. He did not mean to
represent his country at the Congress of Paris, nor did
he hope that any good would come out of it for Italy.
He wished, however, that Sardinia should figure, if not
to her advantage, at any rate with dignity and decorum,
and he turned, as he was wont to do when he wanted a
"perfect knight," to the *rivale*, Massimo d' Azeglio.
Both men had the little private joke of calling one
another by this name in their familiar letters, which
shows how free they were from any real jealousy.
D' Azeglio was ready to accept what had the prospect of
being a most thankless office, but on one condition—
that the Sardinian plenipotentiary should be received on
an equality with the representatives of the great Powers.
Cavour knew that this condition had been explicitly
refused; to please Austria, France and England declared
that Sardinia would only be invited to share in those
sittings of the Congress which affected her interests.
Cavour did not let D' Azeglio know of the refusal; it
was a case of the "tortuous ways of Count Cavour," of
which the Prince Consort complained some years later.
Cavour was scrupulous about the principles which he
considered vital, but in dealing with men, and especially
in dealing with his old colleague, he made more mental
reservations than a severe moralist would allow. In the
present instance the deception failed, for D' Azeglio,
seized at the last moments with suspicions, insisted on
seeing the diplomatic notes which had been exchanged
relative to the Congress. In reading these, he discovered the true state of affairs, and in a violent fit of
anger he refused to go. This incident was the sole cause

of the departure of Cavour himself in the place of his indignant nominee. So are rough-hewn ends shaped.

In January, just before the armistice, Cavour had sent the memorandum on what could be done by the Emperor for Italy, which Napoleon authorised him to write when he was in Paris. The first draft of the document was written by D' Azeglio, in whose literary style Cavour felt more faith than in his own; but this was not used. It was " magnificent," Cavour said, but " too diffuse and long." With the Emperor it was needful to put everything in the most concrete form, and to take a general view of all the hypotheses, except war with Austria, which, " for the present," did not enter into his ideas. D' Azeglio was offended at the rejection of his work. He wrote complainingly, " I may be called a fool about everything else, Amen ; but about Italy, no ! " The memorandum actually sent was short and moderate in tone, the chief point recommended being the evacuation of Bologna by the Austrians. It has been sometimes quoted in order to convict Cavour, at this period, of having held poor and narrow views of the future of Italy. But a man who is mounting a stair does not put his foot on the highest step first. At this stage in his political life most of Cavour's biographers pause to discuss the often-put question, Was he already aiming at Italian unity ? Perhaps the best answer is, that really it does not matter. To be very anxious to prove the affirmative is to misunderstand the grounds on which we may call Cavour one of the greatest of statesmen. Those grounds are not what he hoped to do, but what he did. He was not a Prometheus chained to a rock, who hopes till hope creates the thing it contem-

plates. Constitutionally he was easily discouraged. In
the abstract he rather exaggerated difficulties than
minimised them ; but in the face of any present obstacle
an invincible confidence came over him in his power to
surmount it. As he once wrote of himself—moderate
in opinion, he was favourable, rather than not, to extreme
and audacious means. However long it may have been
before the union of all parts of Italy seemed to Cavour
a goal within the range of practical politics (that he
always thought it a desirable goal there is not the
smallest doubt), there was one, the Tiresias of the old
order, who said boldly to the Prime Minister of Piedmont
at this very juncture : You are steering straight to
Italian unity. Solaro de la Margherita, who once
declared that " in speaking of kings all who had not
sold their consciences were seized with religious terror,"
saw what he would not see, more clearly than it was
seen by those who would have died to make it true.
Standing on the brink of the past, the old statesman
warned back the future. In the debate on the loan for
thirty million francs required to meet the excess in war
expenditure (January 14), Count Solaro said : " The
object, Italian unity, is not hidden in the mysteries of
the Cabinet ; it glimmers out, clear as the light of day,
from the concatenation of so many circumstances that I
lift the veil of no arcanum in speaking of it ; and even
if I did, it would be my duty to lift it and warn all
concerned of the unwisdom and impropriety of those
aspirations." Deny it who would, he continued, unity
was what was aimed at—what was laboured for with
indefatigable activity. Italian unity ! How could it
sound to the other Italian princes ? What was its real

meaning for the Pope? The unity of Italy could only be achieved either by submitting the whole peninsula to the Roman Pontiff or by depriving him of the temporal power. And the speaker ended by prophesying, his only prophecy which failed, that this shocking event would not happen in the present century, whatever God might permit in the next.

An unwary minister would have taken up the ball and thrown it back. Cavour's presence of mind prompted him to leave it where it lay. He did not say, " No, we are not working for Italian unity ; no, we do not wish to overthrow the Pope." He answered that in speaking of the future of Italy it was impossible for a Piedmontese minister to entirely separate his desires, his sympathies, from what he considered his political duty : hence there was no more slippery ground than that on which, with consummate art, the Deputy Solaro de la Margherita had tried to draw him. But, he said, he would avail himself of the privilege generally conceded to the ministers of a constitutional government when questions were still pending—to defer his reply till the case was closed (*a guerra finita*).

CHAPTER VII

THE CONGRESS OF PARIS

WITH the foreboding that this would be the last act of his political life, Cavour started on the mission which he had almost no choice but to assume, in spite of his extreme repugnance for the *rôle* of diplomatist. A few days after his arrival in Paris he was informed that the Emperor, in concert with England, conceded the point as to placing the representative of Sardinia on the same footing as the others. Though it does not seem to have struck Cavour, the sudden change of intention was evidently an involuntary tribute to himself : how could such a man be treated as an inferior ? Only the form was won; the substance remained in doubt. Lord Clarendon hinted to the Piedmontese plenipotentiary that he had "too much tact" to mix in discussions which did not concern him. But Cavour was not discouraged. With his usual quick rebound he was soon thoroughly braced up to the work before him. As he began to see his way, he was rather spurred on than disconcerted by the chorus of dismal predictions which the Congress and his own part in it evoked at home. Almost every notable man in Piedmont contributed his quota of melancholy vaticination, in which the note, "I told you so!" was already audible. Who could plead Italy's cause in a congress in which Austria had a voice? Was there ever such midsummer madness? "But we knew how it would be from the first."

Cavour had said that he hated playing at diplomacy; but some of his smaller, as well as larger gifts, marked him out as a successful diplomatist. He was watchful for little advantages. All who could help the cause were enlisted in its service. Thus he made a convert of a fair Countess, to whose charms Napoleon III. was supposed not to be insensible. Paris was full of notabilities whom he sought to turn into useful allies. In a letter to the Marquis Emanuel d'Azeglio (the Sardinian Minister in London) he tells how he even "made up" to Lady Holland's dog with such success that he got it to put its large paws on his new coat! When the Marchioness of Ely arrived to be present on the part of the Queen at the birth of the Prince Imperial, Cavour, knowing her to be the Queen's intimate correspondent, lost no time in paying his court to her; but in this instance an acquaintance begun from political motives ripened into real friendship on both sides. A point which is worth observing is that, as minister, no one ever made less use of what may be called the influence of society than Cavour. He never tried to make himself agreeable at Turin, least of all to the king. For a long time he was considered haughty by those who did not know him, and arbitrary by those who did. But abroad he underwent a change which probably came about from his revealing not less but more of his natural self. "He has that petulance," Massimo d'Azeglio

said, "which is exactly what they like in Paris."
Abroad he could give this quality freer play than in
Italy, where vivacity offends in a serious man. He
charmed even those who did not share his opinions.
At a dinner given by the Cardinal Archbishop of Paris
to all the members of the Congress, he sat next to the
Abbé Darboy, one day to succeed to the see and meet a
martyr's death in the Commune. The Abbé never
forgot his neighbour of that evening, and in 1870, at
Rome during the Œcumenical Council, when some one
mentioned Cavour's name, he exclaimed, throwing
up his hands, "Ah, that was a man in a thousand!
He had not the slightest sentiment of hate in his
heart."

In the two months which Cavour spent in Paris he
perceived very clearly that Walewski and the other
French ministers would have to be reckoned more as
opponents than friends in the future development of
affairs. He found, however, two men who could be
trusted to continue his work by incessantly pushing
Napoleon III. in an Italian direction ; one was Prince
Napoleon, the other, Dr. Conneau, a person entirely
in the Imperial confidence. Henceforth Dr. Conneau
was the secret, and for a long time quite unsuspected,
intermediary between Cavour and the Emperor. The
idea of establishing this channel of communication first
occurred to Count Arese, whose own influence at the
Tuileries, though exercised with prudent reserve, was
of no slight importance. This Milanese nobleman per-
sonified, as it were, all the proud hatred of the Lombard
aristocracy for an alien yoke. The truest and most
disinterested friend of Queen Hortense, Arese remained

faithfully attached to her son in good and evil fortune. He would never turn the friendship to account for himself. When Napoleon offered to ask as a personal favour for the removal of the sequestration on his family property, he answered that he preferred to take his chance with the rest. He won the lasting regard of the Empress, though she knew that he influenced Napoleon in a sense contrary to her own political sympathies. The visits of this high-minded gentleman and devoted friend were as welcome at a court crowded with self-seekers and charlatans as they were to be later in the solitude of Chislehurst. Arese was in Paris during the Congress, having been chosen by the king, at Cavour's urgent request, to carry his congratulations to the Emperor on the birth of the Prince Imperial.

At the earlier sittings of the Congress, Cavour kept in the background; his instinct as a man of the world, and that mixture of astuteness and simplicity which he shared with many of his countrymen (even those of no education), guided him in filling a difficult and, in some respects, an embarrassing position. He spoke, when he did speak, in as brief terms as could serve to express his opinion. But this modest attitude only threw into relief his inalienable superiority. He cast about the shadow of future greatness. The representative of the second-rate Power, who sat there only by favour, was to make so much more history than any of his colleagues! Curiously enough the only one of the plenipotentiaries who had a prior acquaintance with Cavour was the Austrian, Count Buol, who was formerly ambassador at Turin. In old days, before 1848, he had played whist with him. "I know M. de Cavour," he said; "I am afraid he will give us *du fil à retordre.*" Cavour carefully avoided, however, unnecessary friction. Loyal to both the allies, he managed to steer between their not always consonant aims while preserving his own independence, by taking what seemed, on the whole, the most liberal side in debated questions. With Count Buol he maintained courteous if formal relations, and he soon made a thorough conquest of Count Orloff, who did not begin by being prepossessed in favour of the minister who alone had caused the Sardinian attack on Russia, but who ended on far better terms with him than with his Austrian colleague, of whom he said to Cavour in a voice meant to be heard, "Count Buol talks exactly as if Austria had taken Sebastopol!"

With regard to Cavour's real business, the fate of Italy, he was obliged to proceed with a restraint which few men would have had the self-control to observe. This was what had been predicted; how, in fact, putting aside Austria, could an Italian patriot speak freely of nationality, of alien dominion, of the rights of peoples, in an assembly of old diplomatists, conservative by the nature of their profession and religiously in awe of treaties by the responsibility of their office? It was only just before the signature of peace that Cavour cautiously launched his bolt in the shape of a note on the situation of affairs in Italy, addressed to the English and French plenipotentiaries. It was conceived on the same lines as the letter to Walewski: the Austrian occupation of the Roman Legations was again made a sort of test question, to which particular weight was attached. One reason why Cavour dwelt so much on this point was that the occupation could be assailed on legal grounds, leaving nationality alone.   As, moreover, it was admitted that the Papal Government would fall in Romagna were the Austrians withdrawn, the principle of the destruction of the temporal power of the Pope would be granted from the moment that their departure was declared expedient.   While D' Azeglio thought that the separation of Romagna from the States of the Church would be "positively mischievous," Cavour looked upon it in the light of the first step to far greater changes. Many other schemes were floating in his brain for which he worked feverishly in private, though he did not venture to support them officially.   The object nearest his heart was the union or rather reunion of Parma and Modena with Piedmont, to which those duchies had annexed themselves spontaneously in 1848.   In order to get rid of the Duke of Modena and Duchess of Parma with the consent of Europe, Cavour was desperately anxious to find them—other situations.   Every throne that was or could be made vacant was reviewed in turn ; Greece, Wallachia, and Moldavia, anywhere out of Italy would do ; the Duchess, not a very youthful widow, was to marry this or that prince to obligingly facilitate matters :—abortive projects, which seem absurd now, but Cavour was willing to try everything to gain anything. In weaving these plans Cavour employed the energy of which Prince Napoleon complained that he did not show enough in the Congress, though to have shown more would have led to a rebuff, or, perhaps, to enforced retirement.   Still there was one point which, in the Congress, as out of it, he never treated with moderation : this was the sequestration of Lombard estates.   When Count Buol spoke of an amnesty including *nearly* all cases, he replied that he would not renew diplomatic relations with Vienna while one exception remained. In an audience with the Emperor, after Walewski had ingeniously tried to excuse Austria for exercising her "rights" over her ex-subjects, Cavour burst out with the declaration that if he had 150,000 men at his disposal he would make it a *casus belli* with Austria that very day.

Peace was signed on March 30. A supplementary sitting was held on April 8, when the President, Count Walewski, by express order of the Emperor, and to the astonishment of all present, proposed for discussion the French and Austrian occupations of the Roman States and the conduct of the king of Naples (his own favourite monarch) as likely to provoke grave complications and to compromise the peace of Europe. This was a victory for Cavour, as it was the direct result of his "note," but he was afraid that the discussion of the Roman question would be kept within the narrowest limits in consequence of its affecting France as well as Austria. Walewski wished so to limit it ; he was embarrassed by the analogy of the French in Rome, and by the fear of saying something unflattering of the Pope. But Napoleon would not have risked the discussion at all had he shared his minister's sensitiveness. The truth was, that he was always looking out for an excuse which would serve with the clerical party in France for recalling his troops from Rome. He was thinking then of withdrawing them so as to oblige Austria to withdraw her forces from the Legations. It does not appear that Cavour guessed this. In his own speech he glided over the presence of the French in Rome as lightly as he could, merely saying that his Government "desired" the complete evacuation of the Roman States; but his reserve was not imitated by Lord Clarendon, nor could Napoleon have expected that it would be. When some one asked Lord Palmerston for a definition of the difference between "occupation" and "business," he answered on the spur of the moment—"There is a French occupation of Rome, but they have no business there;" and this witticism correctly represented English opinion on the subject. It was natural, therefore, that the British plenipotentiary should make no distinction between the French in Rome and the Austrians at Bologna: he denounced both occupations as equally to be condemned and equally calculated to disturb the balance of power, but at the root of the matter was the abominable misgovernment, which made it impossible to leave the Pope to his subjects without fear of revolution. The papal administration was the opprobrium of Europe. As to the king of Naples, if he did not soon mend his ways and listen to the advice of the Powers, it would become their duty to enforce it by arguments of a kind which he could not refuse to obey. An extraordinary sensation was created by the speech of which this is a bald summary; it might have been spoken, Cavour said, "by an Italian radical," and the vehemence with which it was delivered doubled its effect. Lord Clarendon, who, at the beginning of the Congress, was nervous as to what Cavour might do, had been worked up to such a pitch of indignation by the private conversations of his outwardly discreet colleague that he himself threw diplomatic reserve to the winds. Walewski, dreadfully uncomfortable about the Pope, tried to bring the discussion back within politer bounds;

Buol was stiffly indignant; Orloff, indifferent about the Pope, was on tenter-hooks as to Russia's friend, the king of Naples; the Prussian plenipotentiary said that he had no instructions; the Grand Vizier was the only person who remained quite calm. Cavour's concluding speech was dignified and prudent; his real comment on the proceedings was the remark which he made to every one after the sitting was over: "You see there is only one solution—the cannon!"

On April 11 he called on Lord Clarendon with the intention of driving home this inference. Two things, he said, resulted from what had passed: firstly, that Austria was resolved to make no concession; secondly, that Italy had nothing to expect from diplomacy. This being so, the position of Sardinia became extremely difficult: either she must make it up with the Pope and with Austria, or she must prepare, with prudence, for war with Austria. In the first alternative he should retire, to make place for the retrogrades; in the second he wished to be sure that his views were not in opposition to those of "our best ally," England. Lord Clarendon "furiously caressed his chin," but he seemed by no means surprised "You are perfectly right," he said, "only it must not be talked about." Cavour then said that war did not alarm him, and, when once begun, they were determined that it should be to the knife (using the English phrase); he added that, however short a time it lasted, England would be obliged to help them. Lord Clarendon, taking his hand from his chin, replied, "Certainly, with all our hearts."

When, after Cavour's death, the text of this conversation was printed, Lord Clarendon denied in the House of Lords having ever encouraged Piedmont to go to war with Austria. Nevertheless, it is impossible that Cavour, who wrote his account of the interview directly after it occurred, could have been mistaken about the words which may well have escaped from the memory of the speaker in an interval of six years. With regard to the sense, the sequel proved that Lord Clarendon did not attach the official value to what he said which, for a moment, Cavour hoped to find in it. Lord Clarendon's speech before the Congress gives evidence of a state of mind wrought to the utmost excitement by the tale of Italy's sufferings, and it is not surprising if, speaking as a private individual, he used still stronger expressions of sympathy. Nor is it surprising that Cavour attributed more weight to these expressions than they merited. Up till now, he had never counted on more than moral support from England; he admitted to himself that the English alliance, which he would have infinitely preferred to any other, was a dream. But the thought now flashed on him that it might become a reality. He decided to pay a short visit to England, which was useful, because it dispelled illusions, always dangerous in politics. In the damp air of the Thames, Lord Clarendon seemed no longer the same enthusiast, and Lord Palmerston pleaded the excuse of a domestic affliction for seeing very little of Cavour. The Queen was kind as ever, but the momentary hope conceived in Paris vanished. One after-consequence of this visit was Lord Lyndhurst's motion, which nearly caused an estrangement between the British and Sardinian Governments. Cavour had taken too literally the assurance that on the subject of Italy there was no division of parties. The warmly

Italian speech of the veteran conservative statesman
which had been inspired by him was not meant to
embarrass the ministry, but that was its effect, and it
was natural that they should feel some resentment.
Fortunately the cloud soon passed away, and if Cavour
imagined to gain anything from flirtations with the Tory
party he was undeceived by the violently pro-Austrian
speech delivered by Mr. Disraeli in July. The sincere
goodwill of individuals such as Lord Lyndhurst and
Lord Stanhope (who invented the phrase "Italy for the
Italians," so often repeated later) did not represent the
then prevailing sentiment of the party as a whole.

Cavour returned to Turin without bringing, as
Massimo d'Azeglio expressed it, "even the smallest
duchy in his pocket"; yet satisfied with his work, for he
rightly judged that, though there was no material gain,
the moral victory was complete. The recalcitration of
Austria, which had reached the point of threatening war
if Parma were joined to Piedmont, contained the germs
of her dissolution as an Italian power. The temporal
power of the Pope had been called in question for the
first time, not in the lodge of a secret society, but in the
council chamber of Europe. Beaten on the lower plane,
Cavour had won on the higher; checked as a Piedmontese, he was triumphant as an Italian. In spite of the
approval voted by both Houses of Parliament, some
shade of disappointment existed in Piedmont, but
throughout Italy there was exultation. The Tuscan
patriots sent the statesman a bust of himself, with the
happily chosen inscription : "Colui che la difese a viso
aperto." [1]

[1] "He who defended her with open face " (Dante).

The position of Piedmont after the Congress of Paris was one to which it would be difficult to find a parallel. States are commonly at peace or at war; if at peace, even where there are smouldering enmities, an appearance is kept up of mutual toleration. But in Piedmont the king, government, and people were already morally at war with Austria. When Cavour said in the Chamber that the two months during which he sat side by side with the Austrian plenipotentiaries had left in his mind no personal animus against them, as he was glad to admit their generally courteous conduct, but the most intimate conviction that any understanding between the two countries was unattainable, he was certainly aware of the grave significance of his words. Great solutions were not the work of the pen, and diplomacy was powerless to change the fate of peoples : these were the conclusions which he brought away from Congress. Every one knew that they meant war. Except for the order for marching, the truce imposed by Novara was broken. Those who had been edified by Cavour's cautious language in Paris stood aghast. It was well enough that Piedmont should protest in a calm, academic way, but protest was now abandoned for defiance. The change was the more unwelcome, because both in France and England the pendulum of the clock was swinging towards Austria. Napoleon disliked to commit himself to any policy, and after seeming to adopt one side he invariably swayed to the other. There was not the same intentional inconsistency in England, but the fact that Austria was undergoing a detachment from Russia improved her relations with England. Lord Palmerston suspected Cavour of being too friendly with Russia. In addition

to this, there was a real fear in England lest Piedmont
should pay dearly for what was considered its rashness.
The British Government put the question to Cavour,
whether it would not be better to disarm the opposition
of Austria by depriving her of every plausible reason
for combating the policy of Piedmont? He replied that
only Count Solaro de la Margherita and his friends
could live on amicable terms with the oppressors of
Italy; England was at liberty to renew her old alliance
with Austria if she chose, but upon that ground he
could not follow her; Lord Palmerston might end where
Lord Castlereagh began, but they would remain faithful
to their principles whatever happened.

Two causes tended to prolong a coldness that was
new in the intercourse between England and Piedmont.
One was the frontier question of Bolgrad, in which, however, Cavour finally acted as mediator, his suggestion being
accepted both by the English and the Russian Governments. The other was the *Cagliari* affair: the *Cagliari*,
a Sardinian merchant ship, which carried the ill-fated
expedition of Pisacane to Sapri, was captured by the
Neapolitan Government, and the crew, two of whom
were English, were taken in chains to Salerno. At first
the English Foreign Office seemed inclined to back up
an energetic demand for restitution, but afterwards it
deprecated strong measures, and left Sardinia somewhat
in the lurch. Circumstances combined, therefore, to
render Cavour isolated, but he understood that this was
a reason to advance, not to retreat. Had Sardinia
seemed to bend to the peaceable advice of her friends
abroad, her ascendency in Italy would have been gone
for ever. Cavour drilled the army, and drew nearer to

those great popular forces that were destined to make
Italy, which could be freed, but never regenerated, by
the sword. Piedmontese statesmen had always looked
askance at these forces; Cavour was becoming fully
alive to the vast motive power they would place in the
hands of the man who could command them, and whom
they could not command. He was free from the caste prejudices which caused many even good patriots of that
date to hold the masses in horror. If he had prejudices
they were against the men of his own order. Once, in
summing up the results of an unsatisfactory general
election, he wrote: "A dozen marquises, two dozen
counts, without reckoning barons and cavalieri—it was
enough to drive one mad!" When he had to do with
men born of the people, he instinctively treated them on
a perfect equality, not a common trait, if the truth were
told. In August 1856 an event took place which had
far-reaching consequences : the first interview between
Cavour and Garibaldi. Cavour was one of Garibaldi's
earliest admirers; he applauded his exploits at Monte-
video and at Rome, when the old Piedmontese party
tried to belittle him and obliged Charles Albert to
decline his services. In one way the hero was a man
after the minister's own heart: he was absolutely practical; he might be obstinate or rash, but he was no
doctrinaire. Cavour never changed his opinion of people,
and even after the General became his enemy he still
admired and esteemed him. In 1856 he received him
with flattering courtesy, the first recognition he had met
with from any person in authority in his own state, from
which, after 1849, he had been, not exactly banished,
but invited to depart. During the same autumn Cavour

began to see much of Giuseppe La Farina, a Sicilian exile, who was intimately connected with the new party, which, despairing alike of the existing governments and of the republic, took for its watchword, "Italy under Victor Emmanuel." In the first instance, La Farina was commissioned to ask Cavour to explain his views. His answer was perfectly frank. He had faith, he said, in the ultimate union of Italy in one state, with Rome for its capital; but he was not sufficiently acquainted with the other provinces to know whether the country was ripe for so great a transformation. He was minister of the king of Sardinia, and he could not and ought not to do anything which would compromise the dynasty. If the Italians were really ready for unity, he had the hope that the opportunity of getting it would not be very long delayed; meanwhile, as not one of his political friends believed in its possibility, the cause would only be injured were it known that he had direct dealings with the men who were working for it. He was willing to receive La Farina whenever he liked, but on the understanding that he came in the morning before it was light, and that, if Parliament or diplomacy got wind of their relations, he should reply that he knew nothing about him. The interviews took place almost daily for four years, without any one knowing of them. Some hours before dawn La Farina ascended the narrow secret staircase which led directly to Cavour's bedroom, and he was gone when the city awakened. In spite of the almost melodramatic complexion of these secret meetings, it must not be supposed, as some have supposed, that Cavour pulled the wires of all the conspiracies in Italy. His visitor kept him informed of the progress

made, the propaganda carried on, but he rarely interfered. He still thought that his own business was
to make Piedmont an object-lesson in constitutional
monarchy, and to get the Austrians out of Italy. That
done, the country, left to itself, must decide whether it
would unite or not.

After the Congress of Paris, Cavour took the Foreign
Office in addition to the Ministry of Finance. He could
not trust either of these departments to other hands;
and the country approved, for the conviction gained
ground that, whether he was mad or not, only he could
extricate it from the situation into which he had drawn
it. When one senator called him a "dictator," he
retorted that, if Parliament refused him its support, he
should go away, which was not the habit of dictators.
But the mere threat of resignation brought the most
recalcitrant to reason. Thus he continued to obtain
large sums to carry out the works he deemed necessary,
one of the greatest of which was the transfer of the
arsenal from Genoa to Spezia—a step which angered
the Genoese on one side, and on the other the old
conservatives, who asked what had little Piedmont to
do with big fleets? "But the fact was," Count Solaro
said with a sneer, "the Prime Minister had all Italy in
view, and was preparing for the future kingdom."
Cavour also forced Parliament to vote the supplies
required for undertaking the boring of Mont Cenis,
which most of the deputies expected would be a total
failure. In proposing this vote he declared that they
must advance or perish. He was delighted with a
phrase with which Lord Palmerston concluded a con-
gratulatory letter sent to the Sardinian legation in

London, and written in elegant Italian : "Henceforth
no one will talk of the works of the ancient Romans."
This little episode wiped out the last traces of misunderstanding between the two statesmen, who became again
what fate had meant them to be, friends and fellow-
workers. Cavour's budgets had the inherent defect
that they continued to show increased expenditure and
a deficit, but no minister who had lacked the power
and the courage to brave criticism by a financial policy
which would have been certainly indefensible if Piedmont
alone was concerned, could have done what he did.
Meanwhile, on the whole, the economic state of the
country improved in spite of heavy taxation : the
exports and imports increased ; there were signs of
industrial activity ; agriculture revived. Cavour was
often bitterly blamed for favouring and sparing the
landowning class, though whether he did this because
he had estates at Leri, as his detractors alleged, or
because agriculture must always be the most vital of all
Italian interests, need not be discussed now. Improved
education stimulated enterprise. That there was room
for improvement may be supposed, when it is known
that in 1848 the number of persons who could not read
was three to one to the number of those who could.

The most severe phase in the financial difficulties
was past when, at the beginning of 1858, Cavour con-
signed the exchequer to Lanza, assuming himself the
Ministry of the Interior, which was vacant through the
resignation of Rattazzi. The breach between the two
men, who were never in entire intellectual harmony,
had been growing inevitable for some months. It was
final ; Cavour resolved never again to have Rattazzi for

a colleague. The elections of the autumn before, which
Cavour thought that Rattazzi had mismanaged, lessened
his confidence in him ; but the actual cause of their
rupture was briefly this.   Cavour wished to put an end
to the king's relations with the Countess Mirafiori, whom
he married by the rite of the Church during his serious
illness near Pisa in 1868—an interference in the private
affairs of the sovereign which, though inspired by regard
for the decorum of the Crown, must be admitted to have
been unwise, as (amongst other reasons) it was certain
not to attain its object.   In this matter Cavour thought
that Rattazzi ought to have stood by him, instead of
which he took the part of the deeply offended king, who
went so far as to say that only his position and his duty
to the country prevented him from challenging his prime
minister then and there.

CHAPTER VIII

THE PACT OF PLOMBIÈRES

TIME seems long to those who wait. The thrill of expectancy that passed through Italy after the Congress of Paris was succeeded by the nervous tension that seizes people whose ears are strained to catch some sound which never comes. Especially in Lombardy there was a feeling of great depression : no one trusted now in revolution, which the watchfulness of the Austrians made as impossible as their careless belief in their own invulnerability had made it possible in 1848. The years went by, and help from without appeared farther off than ever. Meanwhile every interest suffered, and life was rendered wellnigh intolerable by the ceaseless antagonism between government and governed. This was the state of things when the Archduke Maximilian came to Milan full of genuine love for the Emperor's Italian subjects and of determination to right their wrongs. "I much admire M. de Cavour," he said to a Prussian diplomatist, "but when it is a question of a policy of progress, I am not going to let him outdo me." On his side Cavour remarked, "That Archduke is persevering, and will not be discouraged, but I am persevering too, and will not let myself be discouraged." Nevertheless, if there was one thing that Cavour had always feared, it was Austrian conciliation. The gift of a milder rule would change the aspect of the whole question before Europe, and only those ignorant of human nature could suppose that it would entirely fail in its effect with a population which was beginning to be hopeless. Cavour viewed the experiment not without anxiety, but he guessed that the good intentions of Maximilian would be frustrated by the Viennese Government. The forecast was verified, but meanwhile the simple fact that an Austrian archduke had set his heart on winning the affections of the Lombards and Venetians was taken everywhere as a sign favourable to peace.

Then happened the unforeseen event which marks with almost unfailing regularity the turning points in history. On January 14, 1858, Felice Orsini tried to assassinate Napoleon III. and failed. His failure was strange. The bomb thrown under the carriage which conveyed the Emperor and Empress to the opera did not explode. An accomplice was arrested with another in his hand, which he had not time to throw. Many of the passers-by received fatal or serious injuries. Of the previous attempts on Napoleon's life none was prepared with such seeming certainty of success. If others were planned with equal deliberation, could the result be doubted? Napoleon was probably putting this question to himself when he appeared in his box, with an impassible face, while the conspirators on the stage sang the chorus of the oaths in *Guillaume Tell*. Not a cheer greeted the sovereigns, though what had occurred in

the street was immediately known. When the first
report reached Turin, Cavour exclaimed, "If only this
is not the work of Italians!" On receiving the particulars with the name of Orsini, he remembered that this
Romagnol revolutionist had written to him nine months
before, offering his services to whatever Italian Government, "not the Papacy," would place its army at the
disposal of the national independence, and urging the
Sardinian ministers to take a daring course, in which
they would have all Italy with them. Cavour did not
answer the letter, "because it was noble and energetic,
and he thought it unbecoming in him to pay Orsini
compliments." If he had summoned Orsini to Piedmont,
the attempt in the Rue le Peletier would never have
taken place.

No one in Europe was more dismayed by the news
than Cavour, who expected a harvest of embarrassments
for Sardinia, and, worst of all, the permanent ill-will of
Napoleon. The first expectation was speedily realised:
floods of official and unofficial invective were poured
upon the two countries, which were held responsible for
nurturing the plot. In England the counter-blast upset
Lord Palmerston's Government, and in Piedmont the
dynasty itself might have been endangered had not
Victor Emmanuel's sense of personal dignity preserved
him from bending to the rod of imperial displeasure.
Cavour was ready even to forestall the cry for pre-
cautionary measures; the air was full of wild rumours,
and he thought that Victor Emmanuel's days and his
own were threatened, a baseless suspicion, for the most
reckless conspirators in those times accounted regicide
madness in a free country. But he believed it, and for

this reason, as well as from his entirely sincere abhor-
rence of political crime, he was quite in earnest in his
resolve to go as far as the Statute would let him to keep
plotters out of Piedmont. Napoleon, however, affected
to consider the action of the Sardinian Government weak
and dilatory, an opinion which he expressed with vehemence to General Della Rocca, who was sent by the
king to congratulate him on his escape. He hinted that,
if his complaints were not attended to, he should seek
an alliance with Austria. All the pride of the Savoy
blood rose in the veins of Victor Emmanuel: "Tell the
Emperor," he wrote to Della Rocca, " in the terms you
think best, that this is not the way to treat a faithful
ally; that I have never tolerated violence from any one;
that I follow the path of honour, for which I have to
answer to God and to my people; that we have carried
our head high for 850 years, and that no one will make
me bow it; and that, notwithstanding, I desire to be
nothing but his friend." Cavour instructed Della Rocca
to "commit the indiscretion" of reading the letter to
the Emperor word for word. At the same time he wrote
to the Sardinian Minister in Paris "that the king was
ready for the last extremity to save the honour and
independence of the country, and we with him." But
extremities were not needful. Napoleon was always
impressed by the true ring of that ancient royalty which
was the one thing which he could not purchase. He
wrote a conciliatory letter to Victor Emmanuel: "It
was only between good friends that questions could
be treated with frankness. Let the king do what he
could, and not be uneasy." The French Foreign Office
went on scolding through the Legation at Turin, till

Cavour said, with a smile, to Prince de Latour
d'Auvergne, "But it is finished; yesterday the king
had a letter from the Emperor which ends the whole
affair."

A little while after, Cavour received a private communication from Paris containing Orsini's last letter,
and inviting him to publish it in the *Official Gazette*. It
was only then that it began to dawn on him what had
been the real effect of the attempt, and of Orsini's trial,
on the mind of the Emperor. Cavour had none of the
fellow-feeling with conspirators that lurked in Napoleon's
brain, and the idea seemed to him absurd that a man
should be strongly moved by the pleading of his would-be
assassin. Among the royal families of Europe, Orsini's
influence was at once understood, but it was thought to
have its source in fear. It was remarked how, when
the sentence of death was passed, the condemned man,
turning to his counsel, whispered the words of Tasso—

> Risorgerò, nemico ognor più crudo,
> Cenere anco sepolto e spirto ignudo.

"The Italian dagger," wrote the Prince Regent of
Prussia, "has become a fixed idea with Napoleon." Yet
it was not only, and perhaps not chiefly, the fear of being
assassinated that inclined Napoleon to listen to Orsini's
dying prayer, "Free my country, and the blessings of
twenty-five million Italians will go with you!" His
own part in the revolutionary movement of 1831 has
been shown to have been no boyish freak but serious
work, into which he entered with the sole enthusiasm of
his life. "I feel for the first time that I live!" he wrote
when on the march towards Rome. The Romagna was

the hotbed of the Carbonari; all his friends belonged to
the Society, and it must always be held probable that he
belonged to it also.   At any rate the memory of those
days lent dramatic force to the last appeal of the man
who was more willing to go to the scaffold than he was
to send him there.

If this view is correct, it follows that when Napoleon
talked about an Austrian alliance to enforce his demand
for restrictive measures in Piedmont, it was a groundless
threat, such as he was always in the habit of using.   A
month after Orsini's execution, the project of an alliance
between France and Sardinia, and of the marriage of the
king's daughter with Prince Napoleon, reached Cavour
in a mysterious manner, and it is still unknown if it
was sent with the Emperor's knowledge, or by some
one who had secretly ascertained what he was thinking
about.   Cavour showed the draft to the king, but he
did not place much credence in it.   Nevertheless, to
keep Napoleon's attention fixed on Italy, he caused him
to be informally assured that if the worst came to the
worst, Sardinia would go to war with Austria by herself;
the situation was already so strained that almost anything would be preferable to its prolongation.   Cavour
had just induced the Chamber to sanction a new loan for
forty million francs, which suggested that, if others were
apt to use empty threats, he was not.   In June Dr.
Conneau, who was travelling "for his amusement,"
stopped at Turin, where he saw both the king and
Cavour.   Under the seal of absolute secrecy it was
arranged that Napoleon and Cavour should meet "by
accident" at Plombières.   Next month the minister left
Turin to breathe the fresh air of the mountains.   He was

not in high spirits. To La Marmora, the only man besides the king who knew the true motive of his journey, he wrote, "Pray heaven that I do not commit some stupidity; in spite of my usual self-reliance, I am not without grave uneasiness." He succeeded in travelling so privately that he was nearly arrested on arriving at Plombières because he had not a passport: a mysterious Italian coming from no one knew where—no doubt a new Orsini! But one of the Emperor's suite recognised him, and made things straight. He passed nearly the whole of two days closeted with Napoleon, the decisive interview lasting from 11 A.M. to 3 P.M., after which the Emperor took him out alone, in a carriage driven by himself. During this drive the subject of the Princess Clotilde's marriage was broached. Towards the end of the visit, Napoleon said to him, "Walewski has just telegraphed to me that you are here!" The French ministers were, as usual, kept in the dark. It flattered Napoleon's *amour propre* to take into secret partnership a man whose place in history he divined. "There are only three men in Europe," he remarked to his guest; "we two, and then a third, whom I will not name." Who was the third? Bismarck was still occupied in sending home advice that was not taken from the Prussian Embassy at St Petersburg. The saying brings to mind another, attributed to the aged Prince Metternich, "There is only one diplomatist in Europe, but unfortunately he is against us; it is M. de Cavour."

In a long letter to the king, Cavour gave a detailed but probably not a complete account of the interviews at Plombières. It is said that among his papers, which

Ricasoli, his successor in the premiership, gave to his heirs, but which they ultimately restored to the State, there is only one sealed packet—that which relates to this visit. He went by no means certain that the Emperor meant to do anything at all; he came away with great hopes, but still without certainty, for his trust in his partner was limited. He never felt sure whether Napoleon was not indulging on a large scale in the sport of building castles in the air, to which all semi-romantic temperaments are addicted. Still the basis of what bore every appearance of a definite understanding had been established. A rising in Massa and Carrara was to serve as the pretext of war. The object of the war was the expulsion of the Austrians from Italy, to be followed by the formation of a kingdom of Upper Italy, which should include the valley of the Po, the Legations, and the Marches of Ancona. Savoy was to be ceded to France. The fate of Nice was left undecided. To all of these propositions the king had authorised Cavour to agree. The hand of the Princess Clotilde was only to be conceded if it was made a condition of the alliance, which was not the case. Cavour believed, however, that everything depended on gratifying the Emperor's wish, and he strongly urged the king to yield a point which seemed to him of no great importance. Since most princesses made unhappy marriages, what did it matter if Prince Napoleon was a promising bridegroom or not? Victor Emmanuel was persuaded by the "reason of State"; but the sacrifice of his daughter cost him more than Cavour could ever conceive.

Napoleon told his visitor that he felt sure of the

benevolent attitude of Russia, and of the neutrality of
England and Prussia, but he had no illusions as to the
difficulty of the task. The Austrians would be hard to
crush, and unless thoroughly crushed they would not
relax their hold on Italy. Peace must be imposed at
Vienna. To this end at least 200,000 Frenchmen and
100,000 Italians would be necessary. Cavour has been
criticised for acquiescing in the crippled programme of
a kingdom of Upper Italy. What was he to do? Victor
Amadeus II., in his instructions to the Marquis del
Borgo, his minister at the Congress of Utrecht, laid
down the rule : " Aller au solide et au présent et parler
ensuite des chimères agréables." This was the only
rule which Victor Emmanuel's minister could observe
with any profit to his country at Plombières. As he
wrote himself, " In politics one can only do one thing
at a time, and the only thing we have to think of is
how to get the Austrians out of Italy."

The period from the meeting with the Emperor of
the French to the outbreak of the war was, in the
opinion of the present writer, the greatest period in
Cavour's life. Patience, temper, forethought, resource,
resolution—every quality of a great statesman he ex-
hibited in turn, and above all the supreme gift of making
no mistakes. He did not trust in chance or in fate ; he
trusted entirely in himself. He showed extraordinary
ability in compelling the most various and opposing
elements to combine in the service of his ends. In spite
of Napoleon's promises and of the current of personal
sentiment which lay beneath them, he soon foresaw that
the unwillingness of France and the constitutional
vacillation of the Emperor would render them barren of

results, unless Austria attacked—an eventuality which
was considered impossible on all sides. Mazzini, who
was generally not only clear-sighted, but also furnished
with secret information, the origin of which is even now
a mystery, asserted positively that "even if provoked
Austria would not attack." The same belief prevailed
in the inner circle of diplomacy. When Mr. Odo
Russell called on Cavour in December 1858, he remarked
that Austria had only to play a waiting game to wear
out the financial resources of Piedmont, while, on the
other hand, Piedmont would forfeit the sympathies of
Europe if it precipitated matters by a declaration of
war. The only solution would be if the declaration of
war came from Austria; but she would never commit
so enormous a blunder. "But I shall force her to declare war against us," Cavour tranquilly replied, and
when the incredulous Englishman inquired at what time
he expected to bring about this consummation, he
answered, "About the first week in May." Mr. Odo
Russell wrote down the date in his notebook, and
boundless was his surprise when Austria actually declared war a few days in advance of the time prescribed.
This is statesmancraft!

Cavour had always said that an English alliance
would be the only one without drawbacks. Among
these drawbacks he doubtless placed the melancholy
necessity of ceding Piedmontese territory; but that was
not all. There was a peril which would have appeared
to him yet more fatal than the lopping off of a limb,
because it threatened the vital organs of national life:
the risk of an all-powerful French influence extending
over Italy. To ward off this danger it was of the

greatest moment that Italians should join in their own liberation—that not only the Government and the army but patriots of every condition should rally round the country's flag. Though Cavour has been often said to have lacked imagination, it needed the imaginative faculty to discern what would be the true value of the free corps which he decided to constitute under the name of the Hunters of the Alps. With a promise of 200,000 Frenchmen in his pocket, he was yet ready to confront difficulties which he afterwards called " immense," in order to place in the field a few thousand volunteers of whom the heads of the army declared that they would only prove an embarrassment. Cavour listened to no one. He sent for Garibaldi, then at Caprera, and having made sure of his enthusiastic co-operation, he carried out his project without asking the assent of Parliament and without flinching before the most violent opposition, internal and external. Had not Cavour felt so conscious of his strength he would have been afraid of offending Napoleon by "arming the revolution"; but he knew that the best way to deal with men of the Emperor's stamp is to show that you do not fear them. Garibaldi, who never did anything by halves, placed himself and his influence absolutely at Cavour's disposal. " You can tell our friend that he is omnipotent," he wrote to La Farina. He begged the Government to assume despotic power till the issue was decided. Garibaldi did not love the man of the *coup d'état;* but he knew too much about war to miscalculate either the value or the need of the French alliance. Only a small section of the republicans still stood aloof. Cavour had Italy with him. All felt what Massimo

d' Azeglio expressed with generous expansion, " To-day
it is no longer a question of discussing your policy, but
of making it succeed." Cavour had torn open the letter
with impatience, recognising the handwriting. When he
finished reading it his eyes were full of tears. No
one was more whole-hearted in his support of the
minister who exacted of him two most bitter sacrifices
than the king. " The difficulty," Cavour said, " is to
hold him back, not to spur him on." The public, im-
perfectly informed of what was happening or going to
happen, remained calm, for, at last, its faith in the
helmsman was complete. An amusing story is told of
those times. The Countess von Stackelberg, wife of the
Russian minister at Turin, was buying something at a
shop under the Porticoes, when the shopman suddenly
left her and rushed to the door. On coming back he
said with excuses, "I saw Count Cavour passing, and
wishing to know how our affairs are going on, I wanted
to see how he looked. He looks in good spirits, so
everything is going right."

A misunderstanding arose between France and Austria
on a question connected with Servia ; it was in outward
allusion to this that Napoleon said to the Austrian
Ambassador at the reception of the Corps Diplomatique
on New Year's Day, 1859, " Je regrette que les relations
entre nous soient si mauvaises ; dites cependant à Votre
Souverain que mes sentiments pour lui ne sont pas
changés." Whether there was a deliberate intention to
convey another meaning is a matter of conjecture ; at
all events the whole of Europe gave the words an Italian
sense, and Cavour, though taken by surprise, was not
slow to turn them to account. In writing the speech

from the throne for the opening of Parliament, he introduced a paragraph alluding to clouds in the horizon, and
eventualities "which they awaited in the firm resolve to
fulfil the mission assigned to them by Providence." The
other ministers would not share the responsibility of
language so charged with electricity. Cavour then did
one of those simple things which yet, by some mystery of
the human brain, require a man of genius to do them—
he sent a draft of the speech to Napoleon and asked
him what he thought of it? The Emperor answered
that, in fact, the disputed paragraph appeared too strong,
and he sent a proposed alteration which made it much
stronger! The new version ran : "Our policy rests on
justice, the love of freedom, our country, humanity :
sentiments which find an echo among all civilised
nations. If Piedmont, small in territory, yet counts for
something in the councils of Europe, it is because it is
great by reason of the ideas it represents and the
sympathies it inspires. This position doubtless creates
for us many dangers ; nevertheless, while respecting
treaties, we cannot remain insensible to the cries of grief
that reach us from so many parts of Italy." Cavour had
the French words turned into good Italian by a literary
friend (for he always misdoubted his own grammar) ;
one or two expressions were changed ; "humanity" was
left out. Did it savour too much of Mazzini? Victor
Emmanuel himself much improved the closing sentence
by substituting "cry" for "cries." This was the singularly hybrid manner in which the royal speech of
January 10, 1859, arrived at its final form. Much, at
this critical juncture, depended on its effect, and nothing
is so impossible to foretell as the effect of words spoken

before a public assembly. Cavour stood beside the throne watching the impression which each phrase created; when he saw that success was complete, beyond every expectation, he was deeply moved. The ministers of the Italian princedoms could hardly keep their virtuous indignation within bounds. Sir James Hudson called the speech "a rocket falling on the treaties of 1815"; the Russian Minister, waxing poetic, compared it with the shining dawn of a fine spring day. The "grido di dolore," rapturously applauded in the Chamber, rang like a clarion through Italy. And no one suspected whence this ingenious piece of rhetoric emanated!

The French alliance still rested on nothing more substantial than a secret unwritten engagement which Napoleon could repudiate at will. Cavour, who would have made an excellent lawyer, strove his utmost to obtain some more solid bond, for which the marriage-visit of Prince Napoleon offered a favourable opportunity. The connection with one of the oldest royal houses in Europe so flattered the Emperor's vanity that he authorised the bridegroom and General Niel, who accompanied him, to sign a treaty in black and white, binding France to come to the assistance of Piedmont, if that State were the object of an act of aggression on the part of Austria. Possibly, like other people, he thought that no such act of aggression would be made, and that he remained free to escape from the contract if he chose. A military convention was signed at the same time, one of the clauses of which Cavour was fully determined to have cancelled; it stipulated that volunteer corps were to be excluded. He signed the convention, but fought out the point afterwards and gained it, in spite of Napoleon's strenuous resistance. These transactions were intended to be kept absolutely secret, and the French ministers do not seem to have known of them, but somehow the European Courts, and Mazzini, got wind of a treaty having been signed. Different rumours went about: the Prince Consort was informed that Savoy was to go for Lombardy, and Nice for Venetia; others said that Nice was to be the price of the Duchies and Legations. There was a persistent impression that the island of Sardinia was mentioned, which would not merit record but for the general correctness of the other guesses. There is no reference, however, to Sardinia, in the version of the treaty which has since been published, and Cavour indignantly repudiated the idea of ceding this Italian island to France, when the charge of having entertained it was flung at him a year later. Some doubt may linger in the mind as to whether there was not a scheme for giving the Pope Sardinia in return for part or all his territory.

Once again Cavour repeated his demand for yet more money, and this time it was received not, as heretofore, with reluctant submission, but with acclamation. At last people saw what the minister was driving at; only the few who would have disowned the name of Italian voted with the minority. The fifty million francs were quickly subscribed, chiefly in small sums, in Piedmont itself, a triumphant answer to the Paris house of Rothschild, which had declined to render its help. Cavour's speeches on the new loan were, in reality, addressed to Europe, and no one was more skilful in this kind of oratory than he. Without apparent elaboration, each phrase was studied to produce the effect desired. The policy of Piedmont, he said, had never altered since the king received his inheritance on the field of Novara. It was never provocative or revolutionary, but it was national and Italian. Austria was displayed as the peace-breaker, and, as she was pouring troops into Italy and massing them near the Piedmontese frontier, it was easy to exhibit her in that light. After having made Austria look very guilty, Cavour proceeded to lay himself out to conciliate England, whose policy was, at that moment, everything that he wished it not to be ; but he was determined not to quarrel. The Earl of Malmesbury kept him informed of the "real state of Italy," of which he was supposed to be profoundly ignorant. The Lombards no longer desired to be united to Piedmont, and a war of liberation would be the signal of the reawakening of all the old jealousies, while republicans, dreamers, pretenders, seekers of revenge, power, riches, would tear up Italy between them. In the House of Lords, Lord Derby declared that the Austrian was the best of good governments, and only sought to improve its Italian provinces. Cavour concealed the irritation which he strongly felt. Lord Derby's speech, he said, did not sound so bad in the original as in the translation, and, after all, England's apparent change of front came from a great virtue, patriotism. She suppressed her natural sympathies, because she believed that patriotic reasons required her to back up Austria. He repeated to the Chamber what he had often said in private, that the English alliance was the one which he had always valued above all others. It was a remarkable thing to say at a moment when he hoped so much more from

France than from England. But precisely because he hoped to obtain material assistance from France, he was more than ever anxious to remain on good terms with England. He finely resisted the temptation of saying, " We can do without you." After having got the French into Italy, the next thing to do would be to get them out of it, and he foresaw that England would be useful then. Moreover, angry as he was in his heart, he did not doubt that the "suppressed sympathies" would break out again and prove irresistible. They were even breaking out already, for the arrival of the Neapolitan prisoners caused one of those powerful waves of feeling which, in England, always end by influencing the Government.

Meanwhile, Lord Derby's ministry made Herculean efforts to ward off war, in which, by force of traditions that govern all English parties, they had the opposition entirely with them. They begged Austria to evacuate the Papal Legations, and to leave off interfering with the States of Central Italy. They even asked Cavour to help them, by formulating his views on the best means of peaceably improving the condition of Italy. Cavour answered that at the root of the matter lay the hatred of a foreign yoke. The Austrians in Italy formed, not a government, but a military occupation. They were not established but encamped. Every house, from the humblest home to the most sumptuous palace, was closed against them. In the theatres, public places, streets, there was an absolute separation between them and the people of the country. Things got constantly worse, not better. The Austrian rulers in Italy once offered their subjects some compensation for the loss of

nationality in a policy which defended them from the
encroachments of the court of Rome, but the wise
principles introduced by Maria Theresa and Joseph II.
had been cast to the winds.   Unless Austria completely
reversed her policy, and became the promoter of constitutional government throughout Italy, nothing could
save her ; the problem would be solved by war or
revolution.

It ought to have been apparent that, as far as Piedmont was concerned, the control of the situation had
passed out of the hands of the Government.   The youth
of Lombardy was streaming into the country to enlist
either in the army or in the corps of "Hunters of the
Alps," which was now formed.   Cavour looked on this
patriotic invasion with delight ; "They may throw me
into the Po," he said, "but I will not stop it."   Had he
wished, he could not have stopped the current of popular
excitement at the point it had reached.   It was the
knowledge of this, joined to the threatened destruction
of all his hopes, that well-nigh overpowered him when
—at the eleventh hour—in spite of engagements and
treaties, Napoleon seemed to have suddenly decided not
to go to war.   Prince Bismarck once declared that he
had never found it possible to tell in advance whether
his plans would succeed ; he could navigate among
political events, but he could not direct them.   Since
the meeting at Plombières, Cavour had undertaken to
direct events, the most perilous game at which a statesman
can play.   For a moment he thought that he had failed.

CHAPTER IX

THE WAR OF 1859—VILLAFRANCA

ON the whole it can be safely assumed that Napoleon's
hark back was real, and was not a move "pour mieux
sauter." He was not pleased at the cool reception given
in Italy to a pamphlet known to have been inspired by
him, in which the old scheme was revived of a federation
of Italian States under the presidency of the Pope. The
Empress was against war—it was said "for fear of a
reverse." Perhaps she thought already what she said
when flying from Paris in 1870: "En France il ne faut
pas être malheureux." But more than this fear, anxiety
for the head of the Church made her anti-Italian, and,
with her, the whole clerical party. Nor was this the
limit of the opposition which the proposed war of liberation encountered. Though France did not know of the
secret treaty, she knew enough to understand by this
time where she was being led, and with singular
unanimity she protested. When such different persons
as Guizot, Lamartine, and Proudhon pronounced against
a free Italy,—when no one except the Paris workman
showed the slightest enthusiasm for the war,—it is hardly
surprising if Napoleon, seized with alarm for his dynasty,

was glad of any plausible excuse for a retreat. Such an excuse was forthcoming in the Russian proposal of a Congress, which was warmly seconded by England. Austria accepted the proposal subject to two conditions : the previous disarmament of Piedmont, and its exclusion from the Congress. The bearing of the French Ministry became almost insulting; the Emperor, said Walewski, was not going to rush into a war to favour Sardinia's ambition ; everything would be peaceably settled by the Congress, in which Piedmont had not the smallest right to take part. None of the usual private hints came from the Tuileries to counteract the effect of these words.

Cavour was plunged in blank despair. He wrote to Napoleon that they would be driven to some desperate act, which was answered by a call to Paris ; but his interviews with the Emperor only increased his fears. He threatened the king's abdication and his own retire-ment. He would go to America and publish all his correspondence with Napoleon. He alone was respon-sible for the course his country had taken, the pledges it had given, the engagements already performed (by which he meant the consent wrenched from the king to the Princess Clotilde's marriage). The responsibility would be crushing if he became guilty before God and man of the disasters which menaced his king and his country.

The English Government now proposed that all the Italian States should be admitted to the Congress, and that Austria as well as Piedmont should be invited to disarm. On April 17 Cavour sent a note agreeing to this plan. It was a tremendous risk; but it was the only way to prevent Piedmont from being deserted and left to its fate. If Austria also consented, all was lost :

there would be peace. Could the gods be trusted to make
her mad? Cavour's nervous organisation was strained
at a tension that nearly snapped the cord. It is
believed that he was on the brink of suicide. On April
19 he shut himself up in his room and gave orders that
no one should be admitted. On being told of this, his
faithful friend, Castelli, who was one of the few persons
not afraid of him, rushed to the Palazzo Cavour, where
his worst fears were confirmed by the old major-domo,
who said, "The Count is alone in his room; he has burnt
many papers; he told us to let no one pass; but for
heaven's sake, go in and see him at whatever cost."
When he went in, Castelli saw a litter of torn-up papers;
others were burning on the hearth. He said that he
knew no one was to pass and that was why he had
come. Cavour stared at him in silence. Then he went on,
"Must I believe that Count Cavour will desert the camp
on the eve of battle; that he will abandon us all?" And,
unhinged by excitement and by his great affection for
the man, he burst into tears. Cavour walked round the
room looking like one distraught. Then he stopped
opposite to Castelli and embraced him, saying, "Be
tranquil; we will face it all together." Castelli went
out to reassure those who had brought him the alarming
news. Neither he nor Cavour afterwards alluded to
this strange scene.

At the very moment that Cavour thought he had lost
the game, he had won it. On the same day, April 19,
Count Buol,—somewhat, it is said, against his better
judgment, but yielding to the Emperor, who again
yielded to the military party,—sent off a contemptuous
rejoinder to the English proposals. Ignoring all sug-

gestions, the Austrian Minister said that *they would them-selves call upon Piedmont to disarm.* Here, then, was the famous *acte d'agression.* Napoleon could not escape now.

The fact that this happened simultaneously with Sardinia's submission to the will of Europe was a won-derful piece of luck, which, as Massimo d' Azeglio said, could happen only once in a century. When the Austrian Government took the irrevocable step, it did not know yet that the whole onus of breaking the peace would fall upon it. Nor, it must be remembered, did it know the text of the treaty between France and Sardinia, and in view of the French Emperor's recent conduct it may well have become convinced that no treaty at all existed. Hence it is probable that Austria flattered herself that she would only have to deal with weak Sardinia.

The Chamber of Deputies was convoked on April 23 to confer plenary powers on the king. Many deputies were so overcome that they wept. Just as the President of the Chamber announced the vote, a scrap of paper was handed to Cavour, on which were written the words in pencil : " They are here ; I have seen them." It was from a person whom he had instructed to inform him instantly when the bearers of the Austrian Ultimatum arrived. They were come ; angels of light could not have been more welcome ! Cavour went hastily out, while the House broke into deafening cries of " Long live the king ! " He said to the friend who brought the message, " I am leaving the last sitting of the last Piedmontese Chamber." The next would represent the kingdom of Italy.

The Sardinian army to be placed on a peace-footing,

the volunteers to be dismissed, an answer of "Yes" or "No" required within three days—these were the terms of the Ultimatum. If the answer were not fully satisfactory His Majesty would resort to force. Cavour replied that Piedmont had given its adhesion to the proposals made by England with the approval of France, Prussia and Russia, and had nothing more to say. No one who saw the statesman's radiant face would have guessed that less than a week before he had passed through so frightful a mental crisis. He took leave of Baron von Kellersberg with graceful courtesy, and then, turning to those present, he said, "We have made history; now let us go to dinner."

The French Ambassador at Vienna notified to Count Buol that his sovereign would consider the crossing of the frontier by the Austrian troops equivalent to a declaration of war.

Lord Malmesbury was so favourably impressed by Sardinia's docility and so furious with the Austrian *coup de tête* that he became in those days quite ardently Italian, which he assured Massimo d'Azeglio was his natural state of mind; and such it may have been, since cabinet ministers are constantly employed in upholding, especially in foreign affairs, what they most dislike. He hoped to stop the runaway Austrian steed by proposing mediation in lieu of a Congress; but the result was only to delay the outbreak of the war for a week, much to the disadvantage of the Austrians, as it gave the French time to arrive and the Piedmontese to flood the country by means of the canals of irrigation, thus preventing a dash at Turin, probably the best chance for Austria. Baron von Kellersberg and his companion,

during their brief visit, had done nothing but pity "this
fine town so soon to be given over to the horrors of
war." Their solicitude proved superfluous.

For the present the statesman's task was ended. He
had procured for his country a favourable opportunity
for entering upon an inevitable struggle. When
Napoleon said to Cavour on landing at Genoa, "Your
plans are being realised," he was unconsciously fore-
stalling the verdict of posterity. The reason that he
was standing there was because Cavour had so willed it.
In spite of the Emperor's fits of Italian sympathy and
the various circumstances which impelled him towards
helping Italy, he would not have taken the final resolution had not some one saved him the trouble by taking
it for him. As a French student of history has lately
said, in 1859, as in 1849, there was a Hamlet in the case;
but Paris, not Turin, was his abode. Napoleon needed
and perhaps desired to be precipitated. Look at it how
we may, it must be allowed that he was doing a very
grave thing : he was embarking on a war of no palpable
necessity against the sentiment, as the Empress wrote
to Count Arese, of his own country. A stronger man
than he might have hesitated.

The natural discernment of the Italian masses enlightened them as to the magnitude of Cavour's part in
the play, even in the hour when the interest seemed
transferred to the battlefield, and when an emperor
and a king moved among them as liberators. At Milan,
after the victory of Magenta had opened its gates, the
most permanent enthusiasm gathered round the short,
stout, undistinguished figure in plain clothes and spectacles—the one decidedly prosaic appearance in the

pomp of war and the glitter of royal state. Victor
Emmanuel said good-humouredly that when driving
with his great subject, he felt just like the tenor who
leads the prima donna forward to receive applause.

Success followed success, and this to the popular
imagination is the all-in-all of war. Milan was freed,
though the battle of Magenta was not unlike a drawn
one; Lombardy was won, though the fight for the
heights of Solferino could hardly have resulted as it did
if the Austrians had not blundered into keeping a large
part of their forces inactive. Would the same fortune
be with the allies to the end? Cavour does not appear
to have asked the question. He watched the war with
no misgivings. It was to him a supreme satisfaction
that the Sardinian army, which he had worked so hard
to prepare, did Italy credit. He took a personal pride
in the romantic exploits of the volunteers, though for
political reasons he carefully concealed that he had been
the first to think of placing them in the field. He made
an indefatigable minister of war (having taken the office
when La Marmora went to the front). The work was
heavy; the problem of finding even bread enough for
the allied armies was not a simple one. On one occasion
the French Commissariat asked for a hundred thousand
rations to make sure of receiving fifty thousand; the
officer in charge was surprised to see one hundred and
twenty thousand punctually arrive on the day named.
Cavour's thoughts were not, however, only with the
troops in Lombardy. The whole country was in a fer-
ment, and instead of accelerating events the question
now was to keep pace with them.

When Ferdinand II. died, and a young king, the son

of a princess of the House of Savoy, ascended the throne, Cavour invited him to join in the war with Austria. The invitation has been blamed as insincere and unpatriotic, but the best Neapolitans seconded it. Poerio said he was willing to go back to prison if King Francis would send his army to help Piedmont. Faithful to his primary object of expelling the Austrians, Cavour would have taken for an ally any one who had troops to give. Moreover, an alliance between Naples and Sardinia meant the final shelving of a scheme which had caused him anxiety, off and on, for many years : that of a Muratist restoration. Though he had always recognised that, were it accepted by the Neapolitans themselves, it would be impossible for him to oppose it, he understood that to place a Murat on the throne of Naples would be to move in the old vicious circle by substituting one foreign influence for another. There is no doubt that the idea was attractive to Napoleon. One of his first cares after he became Emperor had been to find an accomplished Neapolitan tutor for the young sons of Prince Murat. About the time of the Paris Congress emissaries were actively working on behalf of the French pretender in the kingdom of Naples. The propaganda was in abeyance during the war, because Russia made it a condition of her neutrality that the king of Naples should be let alone, but the simple fact that Napoleon had undertaken to liberate Italy was a splendid advertisement of the claims of his cousin. These considerations tended to make Cavour hold out his hand to the young Bourbon king. There is much evidence to show that the first impulse of Francis was to take it, but the counter influences around him were too strong. When he refused, he sealed his own doom, though the time for the crisis was not yet come.

In Central Italy the crisis came at once.   This had been foreseen by Cavour all along.   At Plombières he made no secret of his expectation that the defeat of the Austrians would entail the immediate union of Parma, Modena, and Romagna, with Piedmont.   Napoleon did not then seem to object.   To him Cavour did not speak of Tuscany, but he expected that there, too, the actual government would be overthrown ; what he doubted was what would happen after.   Many well-informed persons thought that the Grand Duke, who would have maintained the constitution of 1848 but for the threats of Austria, would seize the first opportunity of restoring it.   Fortunately Leopold II. looked beneath the surface : he saw that an Austrian prince in Italy was henceforth an anachronism.   The indignities which he suffered when his Italian patriotism—possibly quite sincere— caused him to be disowned by his relations were not forgotten.   He had no heart for a bold stroke, and the exhortations of the English Government to remain neutral were hardly needed.   If he wavered, it was only for a moment ; nor did he care to place his son in the false position he declined for himself.   The Grand Duke left Florence, openly, at two o'clock on April 27, 1859, carrying with him the personal good wishes of all. The chief boulder in the path of Italian unity was gone, but for reasons internal and external much would have to be done before Tuscany became the corner-stone of New Italy.   The Tuscans clung to their autonomy. Though Victor Emmanuel was invited to assume the protectorate, it was explained that this was only meant

to last during the war. The French Emperor thought
that there was an opening for a new kingdom of Etruria
with Prince Napoleon at the head. All sorts of intrigues
were set afoot by all the great powers except England
to re-erect Tuscany as a dam to stem the flood of unity
midway. Cavour was determined to defeat them. It
was against his rule to discuss remote events. He once
said to a novice in public life, "If you want to be a
politician, for mercy's sake do not look more than a
week ahead." Every time, however, that there arose a
present chance of making another step towards unity,
Cavour was eagerly impatient to profit by it. He now
strove with all the energy he possessed to procure the
immediate annexation of Tuscany to Piedmont. The
object was good, but what he did not see was, that the
slightest appearance of wishing to "rush" Tuscany
would so offend the municipal pride and intellectual
exclusiveness of the polished Tuscans, that the seeds
would be laid of a powerful and, perhaps, fatal reaction.
It was at this critical juncture that Baron Bettino
Ricasoli began his year of autocracy. His programme
was : neither fusions nor annexations, but union of the
Italian peoples under the constitutional sceptre of Victor
Emmanuel. It was Tuscany's business, he said, to make
the new kingdom of Italy. He looked upon himself as
providentially appointed to carry that business into
effect. He was called Minister of the Interior, and he
was, in fact, dictator. When any one tried to overawe
him, his answer was that he had existed for twelve
centuries. He had not wished for foreign help, and he
was not afraid of foreign threats. He often disagreed
with Cavour, and he was the only man who never gave

in to him. When Ricasoli took office he and the republican baker, Dolfi, who was his invaluable auxiliary,
were possibly the only two thorough-going unionists-at-
all-costs in Tuscany; when he resigned it twelve months
later there was not a partisan of autonomy left in the
province. This was the work of the "Iron Baron."

In the other three states, where the first shock to the
power of Austria overturned the Government, there were
no such complicated questions as in Tuscany. Parma
and Modena returned to their allegiance of 1848, and in
Romagna those who were not in favour of an Italian
kingdom were not autonomists but republicans, who
were willing to sacrifice their own ideal to unity. The
revolution in the States of the Church was foiled at
Ancona, and put down with much bloodshed at Perugia:
it is curious to speculate what would have been the
result if it had spread to the gates of Rome, as without
this check it would have done. Cavour sent L. C.
Farini to Modena, and Massimo d'Azeglio to Bologna,
to take over what was called the "protectorate," and
special commissioners were also appointed at Parma and
Florence, but at Florence the real ruler was Ricasoli.

On July 5 Cavour told Kossuth that European
diplomacy was very anxious to patch up a worthless
peace, but still he had no fears. He did not guess that
they were on the verge of seeing realised Mazzini's
prophecy of six months before: "You will be in the
camp in some corner of Lombardy when the peace which
betrays Venice will be signed without your knowledge."
In proportion as Cavour had placed faith in Napoleon's
promises, so great was his revulsion of feeling when he
learnt that on July 6 General Fleury went to the

Emperor of Austria's headquarters at Verona with proposals for a suspension of hostilities. The passionate nature which was generally kept under such rigorous control that few suspected its existence for once asserted itself unrestrained. Those around Cavour were in apprehension for his life and his reason. In spite of all that has been said to the contrary, it is probable that Napoleon's resolution, though not unpremeditated, was of recent date. When he entered Milan, he seems to have really contemplated pushing the war beyond the Mincio; there is proof, however, that he was thinking of peace the day before the battle of Solferino, which disposes of the semi-official story that he changed his mind under the impression left on him by the scene of carnage after that battle. Between the beginning and the end of June, reasons of no sentimental kind accumulated to make him pause. Events in Central Italy had gone farther than he looked for, and his private map of the kingdom of Upper Italy was growing smaller every day. Why was this? He cannot have been seized with a warm interest in the unattractive despotism of the Duke of Modena, or the chronic anarchy kept down by Austrian bayonets at Bologna. But it was becoming apparent that if Modena and Romagna were joined to the new Italian kingdom, Tuscany would come too, and this Napoleon had not expected and did not want. He was clever enough to see that with Tuscany the unity of Italy was made. A great political genius would have said, So be it! Never was there worse policy than that of helping to free Italy, and then deliberately rooting out gratitude from her heart. Whatever Napoleon thought himself, he was alarmed by the news from

France ; the Empress and the clerical party were in despair at the revolution in the Roman States, and the country was indignant at the prospect of an Italy strong enough to have a voice of her own in the councils of Europe.

Besides all this, there was still graver news from Germany. Six Prussian army corps were ready to move for the Rhine frontier. The history of Prussian policy in 1859 has not yet been fully written out, but the gaps in the narrative are closing up. That policy was directed by the Prince Regent, and it gives the measure of the success which would have attended subsequent efforts if the day had not arrived when he surrendered himself body and soul into the hands of a greater man. So much for the present German Emperor's theory that the men in the councils of his grandfather only executed great things because they did their master's will. It is true that William I. aimed at the same end as that which Count Bismarck had already in view, and which he was destined to achieve—the ousting of Austria from Germany, as a preliminary to sublimer doings. But while the Prince Regent would not fight Austria, and hoped to get rid of her by political conjuring, the future Chancellor comprehended that the problem could only be settled by the argument *ferro et igni.* Bismarck's policy in 1859 would have been neutrality, with a certain leaning towards Napoleon. This advice, given by every post from St. Petersburg to Berlin, caused him to be accused of selling his soul to the devil, on which he dryly remarked that, if it were so, the devil was Teutonic, not Gallic.

The Prince Regent tried to prevent the Diet from

going to war, because, in a federal war, Prussia's ruler would only figure as general of the armies of the confederation—which meant of Austria. His plan was to let Austria get into very bad difficulties, and then come forward singly to save her. By means of this "armed mediation" he would be able afterwards to dictate what terms he chose to the much indebted Austrian Emperor. It looked well on paper, but the armistice of Villafranca spoilt everything. The Emperor Francis Joseph did not wish to be "saved." This, and only this, can explain his readiness to make peace when, from a military point of view, his situation was far from desperate. No one knew this better than Napoleon. Before the allied armies lay the mouse-trap of the Quadrilateral, so much easier to get into than to get out of. The limelight of victory could not hide from those who knew the facts the complete deficiency of organisation and discipline which the war had revealed in the French army. According to Prince Napoleon, the men considered their head and their generals incapable, and had lost all confidence in them. Nevertheless they fought well; no troops ever fought better than the French when storming the heights of Solferino, but on the very day after that battle, when the Austrians were miles away in full retreat, an extraordinary, though little known, incident occurred. On a report spreading from the French outposts that the enemy was upon them, there was an universal *sauve qui peut*—officers, men, sick and sound, gendarmes, infantry, cavalry, artillery trains—in one word, every one made off. What would be the effect of a single defeat on such an army?

It must always appear strange that none of these

things struck Cavour. He only saw the immense, immeasurable disappointment. When he rushed to the king's headquarters near Desenzano, it was to advise him to refuse Lombardy and abdicate, or to continue the war by himself. Cavour had never loved the king, or done justice to his statesmanlike qualities; a bitter scene took place between them, which Victor Emmanuel closed abruptly. Afterwards he met Prince Napoleon, who replied to his reproaches, "*Mais enfin*, do you want us to sacrifice France and our dynasty to you?"

At that juncture it was the king, not the minister, to whom the task of pilot fell. Cut to the heart as he was, he kept his temper. He signed the preliminaries "pour ce qui me concerne," and, as on the morrow of Novara, he prepared to wait. The terms on which the armistice was granted seemed like a nightmare : Venice abandoned; Tuscany, Romagna, Modena, to be handed back to their former masters ; the Pope to be made honorary president of a confederation in which Austria was to have a place. Cavour stood before Italy responsible for the war, and when he said to M. Pietri in the presence of Kossuth, "Your Emperor has dishonoured me—yes, dishonoured!" he meant the words in their most literal sense. But the white heat of his passion burnt out the dishonour, and Cavour, foiled and furious, was the most popular man in the country. His grief was so genuine that even his enemies could not call its sincerity in question. In three days he appeared to have grown ten years older. His first thought was to go and get killed at Bologna, if, as was expected, there was fighting there. Then, as always happened with him, he was calmed by the idea of action : "I will take Solaro de la Margherita by one

hand and Mazzini by the other; I will become a conspirator, a revolutionist, but this treaty shall not be
carried out." When he said this, he had resigned office;
he was simply a private citizen, but all the consciousness
of his power had returned to him. Some delay occurred
in forming a new ministry. Count Arese was first called,
but his position as a personal friend of the Emperor dis-
qualified him for the task. Rattazzi succeeded better,
but during the interregnum of eight or nine days Cavour
was obliged to carry on the Government, and it thus
devolved on him to communicate the official order to the
Special Commissioners to abandon their posts. He
accompanied the order by a private telegram telling
them to stay where they were, and work with all their
might for an Italian solution. Farini telegraphed from
Modena that if the Duke, "trusting to conventions of
which he knew nothing," were to attempt to return, he
should treat him as an enemy to the king and country.
Cavour's answer ran: "The minister is dead; the friend
applauds your decision." Aurelio Saffi well said that
"in these supreme moments you would have called
Cavour a follower of Mazzini." The world often thinks
that a man is changed when he is revealing what he
really is for the first time. It suited Cavour's purpose
to appear cool and calculating, but patriotism was as
much a passion with him as with any of the great men
who worked for Italian emancipation.

CHAPTER X

SAVOY AND NICE

THE dissolution of Parliament by Lord Derby in June led to the return of a Liberal majority and the resumption of power by men who were open advocates of Italian unity. Kossuth believed to his last day that this result was due to him, an opinion which English readers are not likely to share. The gain for Italy was inestimable. The Whigs had supported Lord Malmes- . bury in his unprofitable efforts as a peacemaker; but when the war broke out they had no further reason to restrain their natural sympathies. Lord Palmerston especially wished the new kingdom to be strong enough to be independent of French influences. Had the Conservatives remained in office there is no doubt that they would have supported the plan to constitute Venetia a separate state under the Archduke Maximilian, which was regarded with much favour by that Prince's father-in-law, King Leopold, and hence by the Prince Consort. The Liberal Ministry would have nothing to do with it. Napoleon hoped, in the first instance, to shift the onus of stopping the war from himself to the English Government. He wished the programme of

Villafranca to emanate from England; but, as Lord Palmerston wrote to Lord John Russell, why should they incur the opprobrium of leaving Italy laden with Austrian chains and of having betrayed the Italians at the moment of their brightest hopes? In the same letter (July 6), he pointed out that if a single Austrian ruler remained in Italy, whatever was the form of his administration, the excuse and even the fatal necessity of Austrian interference would remain or return. They were asked to parcel out the peoples of Italy as if they belonged to them! The Earl of Malmesbury once remarked that "on any question affecting Italy Lord Palmerston had no scruples." Had the Conservative statesman continued in office six months longer, in spite of his wish to see Italy happy, the "scruples" of which he spoke would have probably induced him to try and force her back under the Austrian yoke. Whether Cavour's life-work was to succeed or fail depended henceforth largely on England. "Now it is England's turn," he said frequently to his relations in Switzerland, where he went to recover his health and spirits. Soon all traces of depression disappeared. While Europe thought that it had assisted at his political funeral, he was engaged not in thinking how things might be remedied, but how he was going to remedy them. It was not the king, Piedmont, Italy, that would prevent the treaty from being carried out; it was "I." The road was cut; he would take another. He would occupy himself with Naples. People might call him a revolutionist or what they pleased, but they must go on, and they would go on.

There exists proof that after Villafranca, Cavour expected Napoleon to demand Savoy and Nice, or at least Savoy, notwithstanding that Venetia was not freed. The Emperor considered it necessary, however, to go through the form of renouncing the two provinces. He is reported to have said to Victor Emmanuel before leaving for Paris, " Your government will pay me the cost of the war, and we shall think no more about Nice and Savoy. Now we shall see what the Italians can do by themselves." Walewski confirmed this by stating that the simple annexation of Lombardy was not a sufficient motive "for demanding a sacrifice on the part of our ally in the interest of the safety of our frontiers," and in August he formally repeated to Rattazzi that they did not dream of annexing Savoy. Sincere or not, these disclaimers released Victor Emmanuel from the secret bond into which Cavour had persuaded him to enter. The contract was recognised as null. Rattazzi was notoriously opposed to any cession of territory, and had he known how to play his game it is at least open to argument that the House of Savoy might have been spared losing its birthright as the Houses of Orange and Lorraine had lost theirs. But his weak policy landed Italian affairs in a chaos which made Napoleon once more master of the situation.

The populations of Central Italy desired Victor Emmanuel for their king—Was he to accept or refuse ? Rattazzi tried to steer between acceptance and refusal. A great many people thought then that acceptance outright would have brought the armed intervention of France or of Austria, or of both combined. The sagacious historian ought not lightly to set aside the current conviction of contemporaries. Those who come

after are much better informed as to data, but they fail
to catch the atmospheric tendency, the beginning-to-
drift, of which witnesses are sensible. The scare was
universal. The British Government sent a formal note
to France and Austria stating that the employment of
Austrian or French forces to repress the clearly expressed
will of the people of Central Italy " would not be
justifiable towards the government of the Queen." Lord
Palmerston made the remark that the French formula
of " Italy given to herself" had been transformed into
" Italy sold to Austria." He grew every day more distrustful of Napoleon, and more regretful that the only
man whom he believed able to cope with him was out
of office.

" They talk a great deal in Paris of Cavour's intrigues," he wrote to Lord Cowley. " This seems to
me unjust. If they mean that he has worked for the
aggrandisement and for the emancipation of Italy from
foreign yoke and Austrian domination, this is true, and
he will be called a patriot in history. The means he
has employed may be good or bad. I do not know
what they have been; but the object in view is, I am
sure, the good of Italy. The people of the Duchies have
as much right to change their sovereigns as the English
people, or the French, or the Belgian, or the Swedish.
The annexation of the Duchies to Piedmont will be an
unfathomable good for Italy at the same time as for
France and for Europe. I hope Walewski will not urge
the Emperor to make the slavery of Italy the *dénoûment*
of a drama which had for its first scene the declaration
that Italy should be free from Alps to Adriatic.
If the Italians are left to themselves all will go well ;

and when they say that if the French garrison were recalled from Rome all the priests would be assassinated, one can cite the case of Bologna, where the priests have not been molested and where perfect order is maintained."

However much Austria might dislike the turn which events had taken in the Centre, it was generally admitted that she would not or could not intervene, even single-handed, without the tacit consent of France, which had still five divisions in Lombardy. The issue, therefore, hung on France. There is no doubt that Napoleon told all the Italians, or presumably Italian sympathisers who came near him, that he "would not allow" the union of Tuscany with Piedmont. He said to Lord Cowley, "The annexation of Tuscany is a real impossibility." He told the Marquis Pepoli that if the annexations crossed the Apennines, unity would be achieved; and he did not want unity : he wanted only independence. Walewski echoed these sentiments, and in his case it is certain that he meant what he said. But did Napoleon mean what he said ? Evidence has come to light that all this time he was speaking in an entirely different key whenever his visitor was a reactionist or a clerical. To these he invariably said that he was obliged to let events take their course, though contrary to his interests ; because, having given the blood of his soldiers for Italian independence, he could not fire a shot against it. To M. de Falloux he said that he had always been bound to the cause of Italy, and it was impossible for him to turn his guns against her. What becomes, then, of his threats ? Might not an Italian minister, relying on the support of England, have ignored them and passed on his way ?

Though Rattazzi's timidity prevented Victor Emmanuel from accepting the proferred crowns, the king
declared on his own account that if these people who
trusted in him were attacked, he would break his
sword and go into exile rather than leave them to their
fate. He wrote to Napoleon that misfortune might
turn to fortune, but that the apostasies of princes were
irreparable. The Peace of Zurich, signed on November
10, did nothing to relax the strain. It merely referred
the settlement of Italy to the usual Napoleonic panacea
—a Congress not intended to meet. A Congress would
have done nothing for Italy, but neither would it have
given Napoleon Savoy and Nice. But the proposal had
one important result: it brought Cavour back on the
scene. A duel was going on between him and Rattazzi.
He was accused, perhaps truly, of moving heaven and
earth to upset the ministry, while Rattazzi's friends
were spreading abroad every form of abuse and calumny
to keep him out of office. When the Congress was
announced, the popular demand for the appointment of
Cavour as Sardinian plenipotentiary was too strong to
be resisted. Rattazzi yielded, and the king, though still
remembering with bitter feelings the scene at Villafranca,
sacrificed his pride to his patriotism. Cavour did not
like the idea of serving under Rattazzi, but he agreed
to accept the post in order to prevent an antagonism
which would have proved fatal to Italy. Napoleon
astutely uttered no word of protest.

The Congress hung fire, and Cavour remained at
Leri occupied with his cows and his fields, but secretly
chafing at the sight of Italy in a perilous crisis abandoned
to men whom he believed incapable. From the moment

that he had been called back to the public service, his own return to the premiership could only be a question of time, and he wished that time to be short. The fall of the ministry was inevitable, for it was unpopular on all sides, but no one had foreseen how it would fall. La Marmora, who was the nominal president of the Council (Rattazzi having taken his old post of Home Minister), somehow discovered that a draft of Cavour's letter of acceptance of the appointment of plenipotentiary existed in Sir James Hudson's handwriting. Though it was true that the British Government was most anxious that Cavour should figure in the Congress, if there was one, the fact that Sir James Hudson had written down a copy of the letter as it was composed was only an accident which happened through the intimate relations between them. La Marmora saw it in a different light, and angrily declaring that he would not put up with foreign pressure, he sent in his resignation, which was accepted. Thus in January 1860 Cavour became once more the helmsman of Italian destinies. The new ministry consisted principally of himself, as he held the home and foreign offices, as well as the presidency of the Council.

He was resolved to put an end to the block at all costs, except the reconsignment of populations already free to Austria or Austrians. "Let the people of Central Italy declare themselves what they want, and we will stand by their decisions come what may." This was the rule which he proposed to follow, and which he would have followed even if war had been the consequence. Personally he would have accepted a provisional union of the Central States, such as Farini advocated; but

Ricasoli discerned in any temporary division a danger
to Italian unity, and induced or rather forced Cavour to
renounce the idea. He called Ricasoli an "obstinate
mule," but he had the rare gift of seeing that the strong
man who opposed him in details was to be preferred to
a weak man who was only a puppet.

The substitution of Walewski by Thouvenel at the
French Foreign Office, and the Emperor's letter to the
Pope advising him to give up the revolted Legations of
his own accord, raised many hopes, but those who took
these to be the signs of a decided change of policy were
mistaken. Napoleon would not yield about Tuscany,
and it grew plainer every day that the reason why he
held out was in order to sell his consent. M. Thouvenel
has distinctly stated that at this period the English
ministry were informed of the Emperor's intention
to claim Savoy and Nice if Piedmont annexed any more
territory. Even before he resumed office, Cavour was
convinced that the only way to a settlement was to
strike a direct bargain with Napoleon. He viewed the
contemplated sacrifice not with less but with more
repulsion than he had viewed it at Plombières. The
constant harassing of the last six months, which provoked him to say that never would he be again an
accessory to bringing a French army into Italy, left an
ineffaceable impression on his mind. The cession of the
two provinces seemed to him now much less like obliging a friend than satisfying a highwayman. But he was
convinced that it was an act of necessity.

As the "might-have-beens" of history can never be
determined, it will never be possible to decide with
certainty whether Cavour's conviction was right or

wrong. Half a year of temporising had prejudiced the position of affairs ; it was more difficult to defy Napoleon now than when he broke off the war without fulfilling his promises. A clear-sighted diplomatist, Count Vitzthum, has given it as his opinion that if Cavour had divulged the Secret Treaty of January 1859, by which Savoy and Nice were promised in return for the French alliance, Napoleon would have been so deeply embarrassed that he would have relinquished his claims at once. But such a course would have mortally offended France as well as the Emperor. Cavour did not share the illusion of the Italian democracy that the "great heart" of the French nation was with them. He once said that, if France became a republic, Italy would gain nothing by it—quite the contrary. With so many questions still open, and, above all, the difficult problem of Rome, he feared to turn the smothered animosity of the French people into violent and declared antagonism.

The king offered no fresh opposition ; he said sadly that, as the child was gone, the cradle might go too. When the exchange of Savoy for a French alliance was proposed to Charles Albert he wrathfully rejected the idea ; and if Victor Emmanuel yielded, it was not that he loved Savoy less but Italy more. It has to be noticed, however, that, though always loyal to their king, the Savoyards had for ten years shown an implacable hostility to Italian aspirations. The case against the cession of Nice was far stronger. General Fanti, the minister of war, threatened to resign, so essential did he hold Nice to the defence of the future kingdom of Italy. The British Government also insisted on its military

importance. Nice was a thoroughly Italian town in race
and feeling, as no one knew better than Cavour, though
he was forced to deny it. According to an account
published in the *Life of the Prince Consort*, and seemingly
derived from Sir James Hudson, it would appear that
he was still hoping to save Nice, when Count Benedetti
arrived from Paris with the announcement that, if the
Secret Treaty were not signed in its entirety, the Emperor
would withdraw his troops from Lombardy. Cavour is
said to have answered, "The sooner they go the better"
—on which Benedetti took from his pocket a letter
containing the Emperor's private instructions, and proceeded to say, "Well, I have orders to withdraw the
troops, but not to France; they will occupy Bologna
and Florence." [1]

On March 24, depressed and bowed, Cavour walked
up and down the room where the French negotiators
sat. At last, taking up the pen, he signed the Secret
Treaty. Then suddenly he seemed to recover his spirits,
as, turning to M. de Talleyrand, he said, "Maintenant
nous sommes complices, n'est ce pas vrai?"

The secrecy was none of his seeking; he had tried
hard to induce Napoleon to let the treaty be submitted
to Parliament before it was signed, as constitutional
usage demanded, but the Emperor was resolved that the
Chambers and Europe should know of it only when it
was an accomplished fact. He had good reason for the
precaution. He knew that there would be an outburst
of indignation in England, though he little imagined the

---

[1] In 1896 Count Benedetti contributed two articles to the *Revue
des deux mondes* on "Cavour and Bismarck." His only mention
of the affair of Savoy and Nice is the casuistical remark that
"Cavour kept the *engagement concluded at Plombières*" (sic).

after consequences of this to himself. His one idea just then was to make sure of his bargain, not because he cared to enlarge his frontiers, for he was not constitutionally ambitious, but because he hoped, by doing so, to win the gratitude of France. It is useful as a lesson to note that he won nothing of the kind. Nor did Cavour win the goodwill of the French masses as he had hoped. France might have been angry had she not received the two provinces, but she showed real or affected ignorance of their value. For many years the French papers described the county of Nice as a poor, miserable strip of shore, and the duchy of Savoy as a few bare rocks. French people then travelled so little that they may have thought it was true.

As Napoleon was bent on deceiving, Cavour was obliged to deceive too. Sir Robert Peel's denial of the intention of Government to repeal the Corn Laws has been defended on the ground that the *Cabinet* had not taken a definite resolution; if such a defence is of profit, Cavour is entitled to the benefit of it. At any rate he had no choice. Whether or not they had been previously warned, the English Ministry, and especially the Foreign Secretary, now believed the professions of innocence. The Earl of Malmesbury records a suspicion that as far back as January 1859 Napoleon secured some sort of written promise from Lord Palmerston that he would not make difficulties about Nice and Savoy. Such an assurance amounts, of course, to saying, "Go and take it," as in the more recent case of Tunis. The story is not impossible; like Cavour, Lord Palmerston desired so much to see Italy freed that he would have given up a good deal to arrive at the goal. The country resented

the deception, as it had every right to do, and the Queen
expressed the general feeling when she wrote to Lord
John Russell, "We have been made regular dupes."
For a moment there seemed a risk of war, but Lord
Palmerston never had the slightest intention of going to
war, whatever were the inclinations of his colleague
at the Foreign Office. Lord John Russell took his
revenge on Napoleon when the Emperor wished to
proceed to joint action with England on the Danish
question; by refusing this proposal he deprived him
of the one and only chance of stemming Prussian
ambition.

Cavour did not extenuate the gravity of the responsibility which he accepted when he advised the king to
sign away national territory without the sanction of
Parliament. He said that it was a highly uncon-
stitutional act, which exposed him, were the Chamber of
Deputies to disown it, to an indictment for high treason.
He counted on losing all his popularity in Piedmont—
how could he not expect to lose it when his best hopes
for getting the treaty approved rested on the assumption
that the new voters from the enfranchised parts of Italy
would drown the opposition of his own State to its dis-
memberment? It has often been asked, Why did he not
allow the cession to wear the honest colour of surrender
to force? Why, "against his conviction," as he con-
fessed in private, did he declare that Nice was not
Italian? Why go through the farce of plebiscites so
"arranged" that the result was a foregone conclusion?
The answer, satisfactory or not, is easily found: Nice
was stated to be not Italian to leave intact the theory of
nationality for future use; the plebiscites were resorted

to that Napoleon might be obliged to recognise the same method of settling questions elsewhere.

The parliament which represented Piedmont, Lombardy, Parma, Modena, and Romagna, met on April 2, 1860. The frontier lines of six states were effaced. The man who had so largely contributed to this great result stood there to defend his honour, almost his life. Guerrazzi compared him to the Earl of Clarendon— "hard towards the king, truculent to Parliament, who thought in his pride that he could do everything." Cavour retorted: perhaps if Clarendon had been able to show in defence of his conduct many million Englishmen delivered from foreign yoke, several counties added to his master's possessions, Parliament would not have been so pitiless, or Charles II. so ungrateful to the most faithful of his servants. The deputy Guerrazzi, he continued, had read him a lesson in history; it should have been given entire. And he then drew a picture, splendid in its scathing irony, of the unscrupulous alliance of men without principle, of all shades of opinion, only united in self-interest, demagogues, courtiers, reactionists, papists, puritans, without traditions, without ideas, at one in impudent egotism, and in nothing else, who formed the cabal which ruined Clarendon. Every one understood that he was painting his own enemies inside the Chamber and out.

In spite of protests and regrets, the treaty was sanctioned by a larger majority than had been reckoned on. When it came to the point, not a large number of voters was ready to take the tremendous leap in the dark which, among other consequences, must have condemned Cavour, if not to the fate of Strafford, at least to obscurity for the rest of his life. But the ministry came out of the contest, to use Cavour's own words, extraordinarily weakened. "On me and on my colleagues," he had said, "be all the obloquy of the act!" He was to regain his power, and even his popularity, but time itself cannot wholly obliterate the spot upon his name. He knew it well himself. A writer in the *Quarterly Review*, soon after his death, related that latterly people avoided alluding to Savoy and Nice before him; the subject caused him such evident pain. The same writer makes a very interesting statement which, although there is no other authority for it, must be assumed to rest on accurate information: he says that Cavour hoped, to the last, some day to get the two provinces back.[1]

[1] Mr. John Murray has courteously informed me that the writer of the article was the late Sir A. H. Layard.

CHAPTER XI

THE SICILIAN EXPEDITION

IN March 1860 Cavour did not foresee what would be the next step—he only felt that it would not be long delayed. Italy, he told the Chamber, was not sound or safe; Italy had still great wounds in her body. "Look beyond the Mincio, look beyond Tuscany, and say if Italy is out of danger!" He interpreted the transaction with Napoleon in the sense that, whatever happened henceforward, he was to have a free hand. Napoleon seemed to think, at the first, that the cession of Nice and Savoy showed a yielding mood; he was mistaken; it shut the door on yielding. Cavour found all sorts of excuses for protracting the date of the official handing over of those provinces, and this helped him in his dealings with the Emperor, whom he compelled to shelve a particularly obnoxious project of introducing Neapolitan troops into the Roman States. Napoleon was induced to promise to withdraw the French in July without calling in others, on condition, however, that all remained quiet. All was not going to remain quiet.

There were no illusions on this point at the Vatican,

where no one believed that the *status quo* would last. It seemed to many of the Pope's advisers that, instead of waiting for the blow, it were better to strike one, and declare a holy war for thrones and altars. Cardinal Antonelli, in concert with the dominant party at Naples (which was that of the king's Austrian stepmother), evolved a scheme for recovering Romagna, in which it was hoped that Austria would join, Austrian aid being at all times far more desired than French. But the more ardent spirits were not averse from action even without Austria. The Orleanist general Lamoricière was invited to Rome, and a call was issued which brought an influx of Irish and French volunteers. The French Emperor let Lamoricière go, as he was glad to get him out of the way. The Duke de Persigny told his master that the gallant general would make trouble for him in Italy, and, as Napoleon turned a deaf ear, he suggested that Lamoricière should be ordered to garrison Rome while the French regular troops were sent to protect the frontier. This simple arrangement would have commended itself to any one who was in earnest in wishing to preserve the integrity of what remained of the Papal States; Napoleon seemed to assent, but he allowed the matter to drop.

It began to be clear that the Neapolitan Government would soon have too much on its hands at home for it to indulge in crusades. But the crisis was not hastened by Cavour, and he was one of the last to believe it imminent. Towards the end of March he learnt with surprise from Sir James Hudson that the reason the British Fleet had been sent to Naples was that a catastrophe was expected. He then asked the Sardinian

Minister at the Neapolitan Court whether a Muratist restoration was still possible, and what chances there were at Naples for Italian unity? The Marquis Villamarina replied that the French, who once had many partisans, had lost most of them. As to unity he held out few hopes; it was popular in Sicily but not on the mainland, where the king had a strong following. If the Marquis had said "large" for "strong" his assertion would have been accurate. The misgovernment, which Lord John Russell had lately described as almost without a parallel in Europe, was not of a nature to be wholly unpopular; it was national after a fashion; bribery and espionage and the persecution of the best citizens may leave the masses content, and, in fact, at least in the capital, the *basso popolo* was royalist, as was the scarcely less ignorant nobility. The bulk of the clergy and the army was also loyal. All this support made the Bourbon *régime* look not insecure to those on the spot, who failed to understand the complete rottenness of its foundations.

When a revolutionary movement broke out in Sicily, Cavour thought of sending secretly a Piedmontese officer, who fought in the Sicilian insurrection of 1848, to assume the direction, but he did not do so, perhaps because he had very little faith in the success of the attempt. Save for the undoubted fact that Sicily was already separated in spirit not only from the Bourbon crown but from any rule which had its seat at Naples, the insurrection did not begin under promising circumstances. There were no signs of a concerted rising on a large scale, such as had overthrown the Government in 1848, and the authorities disposed of overwhelming means, if they knew how to use them, of crushing a few guerrilla bands. Cavour was slow to believe the catastrophe at hand, but he thought that the time was come to send the King of Naples a warning, which was practically an ultimatum. On April 15 Victor Emmanuel addressed a letter to Francis II., in which he told his cousin that there was possibly still time to save his dynasty, but that time was short. Two things must be done : the first was to restore the Constitution (this even Russia was advising); the second, that the kings of Sardinia and Naples should divide Italy between them, drive out the last Austrian, and constrain the Pope, in whatever strip of territory was left to him, to govern on the same liberal basis as themselves. If these things were not done, and at once, Francis would have the fate of his relative Charles X., and the King of Sardinia might be forced to become the chief instrument of his ruin. It cannot be said that the warning was not sufficiently explicit.

As the insurrection dragged on, the idea gained ground in North Italy of sending out reinforcements to the hard-pressed insurgents. Landings on the southern coast had an unfortunate history from that of Murat downwards, but those who play at desperate hazards cannot be ruled by past experience. Cavour seems to have lent some material aid to a Sicilian named La Masa, who was preparing to take a handful of men to his native island, but it is not true that he either desired or abetted the expedition of Garibaldi. A Garibaldian venture could not be kept quiet; it would raise complications with the Powers, and, besides, what if it failed and cost Garibaldi his life ? Some people have supposed that Cavour sent Garibaldi to Sicily to get rid of him at an awkward moment, for the General was planning a revolutionary stroke at Nice to resist the annexation. Though this theory sounds plausible, documentary evidence is all against it. Cavour had an interview with the Garibaldian general, Sirtori, to whom he expressed the conviction that if they went they would be all taken. Why, it may be asked, did he not stop the whole affair by placing Garibaldi under lock and key? It seems certain that only the king's absolute refusal prevented this effectual measure from being resorted to. The king, accompanied by Cavour, was paying a first visit to Tuscany; there were rumours of stormy scenes between them on the subject of the arrest, and Victor Emmanuel had his way. Whatever was their disagreement, it ceased when the die was cast. It was one of Cavour's chief merits that he instantly grasped a new situation. To let the expedition go and then place obstacles in its way would have been an irreparable mistake. Admiral Persano inquired whether he was to stop the steamers carrying the Thousand to Sicily, should stress of weather drive them into a Sardinian port? The answer by telegraph ran, "The Ministry decides for the arrest." Persano rightly judged this to mean that Cavour decided against it, and he telegraphed back, "I have understood."

Garibaldi sailed from Quarto late on May 5. Not Cavour himself had thought worse of the plan than he when it was first proposed to him, but, with the decision to go, doubt vanished. "At last," he wrote, "I shall be back in my element—action placed at the service of a great idea." No one seems to have pointed out the

extraordinary boldness of choosing a fortified town of
18,000 inhabitants as the place of landing. The leaders
of similar expeditions have always selected some quiet
spot where they could land undisturbed, and the coast
of Sicily presents many such spots. If Garibaldi had
done the same he would have failed, for the success of
the Thousand was a success of *prestige*. Italian patriots
at home had some uneasy days. Victor Emmanuel,
as he afterwards admitted, was in "a terrible fright";
Cavour went about silent and gloomy. A week passed,
and no news came. On May 13, at eleven o'clock at
night, a passer-by in the Via Carlo Alberto, not far
from the Palazzo Cavour, heard some one gaily whistling
the air

" Di quella pira . . . "

Of a sudden the individual, who was walking very
quickly, vigorously rubbed his hands. The trait revealed the man—it was Cavour; he had just heard that
Garibaldi, eluding the Neapolitan fleet, had disembarked
with all his men at Marsala. Things were entering a
new and critical phase, and it was not difficult to foretell
that, while the hero would have all the laurels, the
statesman would have all the thorns. This was a small
matter to Cavour: they were again on the high seas, he
said cheerfully, but what was the good of thinking of
peace and quiet till Italy was made?

The Sardinian Government adopted the policy of
assisting the expedition now as far as they could without
being compromised with the Powers of Europe—but no
farther. This *via media* had the merit of succeeding;
it was, however, severely criticised by friends and foes
at the time. On May 24 Prince Napoleon said in the

presence of Marshal MacMahon, Prosper Mérimée, N. W. Senior, and others, that Cavour had done too much or too little; he should have kept Garibaldi back, or given him 5000 men; he had thrown on himself and on "my father-in-law" all the discredit of favouring the enterprise, and he would have been no more blamed and hated if he had given it real support. On higher grounds Massimo d' Azeglio was horrified at the lack of straightforwardness in mining the Bourbon edifice from below instead of declaring war. "Garibaldi has no minister at Naples, and he has gone to risk his skin, and long life to him, but we!!" Taking this view, the immaculate Massimo, as governor of Milan, impounded a number of rifles intended for the Thousand, and so nearly wrecked the affair. The King of Naples naturally applied the same criticism. "Don Peppino," he said, "had clean hands, but he was only a blind, behind which was ranged Piedmont with the Western Powers, which had vowed the end of his dynasty." Whether international law was violated or not, there was no real deception, if the essence of deception is to deceive, for the Neapolitan Government saw Cavour's hand everywhere, even where it was not.

Cavour was deterred from declaring war by the fear of foreign intervention. England was the only Power which applauded the drama enacting in Sicily. The cover afforded by English ships to the landing of Garibaldi was no doubt a happy accident, but, as Signor Crispi often repeats to this day, the landing could hardly have taken place without it. "C'est infâme et de la part des Anglais aussi," the Czar wrote on the telegram which announced the safe arrival of the "brigands" at Marsala. Cavour was afraid lest Russian sympathy with the court of Naples should take a more inconvenient form than angry words. Russia, however, remained quiescent, though "geography" was stated to be the only reason. Prussia also discovered that Naples was some way off. Yet there was nothing which the Prince Regent so disliked as to see kings overthrown, until he began to do it himself. But the two Northern Powers (and this was the meaning of the talk about geography) did not want to act without Austria. The Austrian Queen Dowager did all she could to obtain help to save the crown, which she expected would pass from the weakly Francis to her own son, but public opinion in Austria had long been irritated by the supineness and corruption of the Neapolitan *régime*, and though the Government protested, it did not go to the rescue. It is a question whether it would not have been forced to go, if, at the outset, Cavour had declared war. France joined in the protests of the other Powers, and Cavour's enemies spread a monstrous rumour that he was going to give up Genoa to win Napoleon's complaisance. In reply to an anxious inquiry from the British Government, he declared that under no circumstances would he yield another foot of ground.

When Garibaldi visited Admiral Persano's flag-ship at Palermo, he was received with a salute of nineteen guns, which practically recognised his position as dictator, and Medici's contingent of 3000 men was equipped and armed by Cavour ; all secrecy as to the relations between the minister and the Sicilian revolution was, therefore, at an end. He wished that Sicily should be annexed at once. Though Garibaldi had performed every act since

he landed in Sicily in Victor Emmanuel's name, Cavour
was more and more afraid of the republicans in his
camp. He exaggerated their influence over their leader,
who, in vital matters, was not easy to move, and he did
not believe that, in accordance with Mazzini's instructions, they were working for unity regardless of the
form of government which might follow.   Victor
Emmanuel could sound the depths of Mazzini's
patriotism ; Cavour never could. The two men were
made to misunderstand each other. There are differences
too fundamental for even imagination to bridge over.
Had they lived till now, when both are raised on
pedestals in the Italian House of Fame, from which time
shall not remove them, Mazzini would still have been
for Cavour, and Cavour for Mazzini, the evil genius of
his country.

The nightmare of Red Republicanism taking the bit
between its teeth and bolting was not the only terror
that disturbed Cavour's rest. He shuddered at the
establishment of a dictatorial democracy which placed
unlimited power in the hands of men of no experience,
with only the lantern of advanced Liberalism to guide
them.   He, who had tried to make the Italian cause
look respectable, as well as meritorious, asked himself
what these improvised statesmen would do next ?   The
Garibaldian dictatorship has not lacked defenders, and
two of its administrators lived to be prime ministers of
Italy, but it was inevitable that Cavour should judge it
as he did.

A dualism began between Palermo and Turin, which
would not have reached the point that it did reach, if La
Farina, who was commissioned by Cavour to promote

annexation, had not launched into a furious personal warfare with his fellow-Sicilian Crispi, a far stronger combatant than he.   Garibaldi ended by putting La Farina on board a Sardinian man-of-war, and begging the admiral to convey him home.   The dictator bombarded the king's Government with advice, to which Cavour alludes without irritation : "He writes and re-writes, and telegraphs night and day, urging us with counsels, warnings, reproaches—I might almost say menaces."   Garibaldi, he goes on to say, has a generous character, poetic instincts, but his is an untamed nature, on which certain impressions leave ineffaceable traces ; he feels the cession of Nice as a personal injury, and he will never forgive it.   The king has a certain influence over him, but it would be madness to seek to employ it in favour of the Ministry ; he would lose it, which would be a great misfortune.   How few ministers who, like Cavour, were accustomed to be all-powerful, would have met unrelenting opposition in this spirit !

The influence of the king was sought by Napoleon to induce Garibaldi to stop short at Messina, but he can hardly have been surprised when the General showed no disposition to serve his sovereign so ill as to obey him. He then proposed that the French and British admirals should be instructed to inform Garibaldi that they had orders to prevent him from crossing the straits.   Lord John Russell replied that, in the opinion of Government, the Neapolitans should be left to receive or repel Gari-baldi as they pleased ; nevertheless, if France interfered alone, they would limit themselves to disapproving and protesting.   But Napoleon did not wish to interfere alone ; the effect would be to make British influence

paramount in Italy, and possibly even to cause Sicily to
crave a British protectorate.   In great haste he assured
the Foreign Secretary that his chief desire was to act
about Southern Italy in whatever way was approved by
England.   Italy was saved from a great peril in 1860,
firstly, by English goodwill, and, secondly, by the absence
of any real agreement between the Continental Powers.
Had there been a concert of Europe, the passage of
Garibaldi to Calabria would have been barred.

By this time no one was more determined than
Cavour himself that not a palm of ground should be left
to the Bourbon dynasty, but he still thought it necessary
to save appearances.   Thus he met the too late advances
of the Neapolitan Government, not by a refusal to treat,
but by proposing a condition with which Francis, as an
obedient son of the Church, could not comply : the
formal recognition of the union of Romagna with Piedmont.   Strict moralists, like Lanza, would have wished
him to send the ambassadors of the King of Naples
about their business, and to declare war on any pretext,
and so escape from "a hybrid and perilous game."
Cavour looked upon the Neapolitan Government as
doomed, and that by its own fault, its own obstinacy,
its own rejection of the plank of safety, which, almost at
the risk of doing a wrong to Italy, he had advised his
king to offer it three months before.   He felt no
scruples in accelerating its fall.   The means he took
may not have been the best means, but he thought them
good enough in dealing with a system which was a by-
word for bad faith and corruption.   He wished that the
end might come before Garibaldi crossed the straits, or,
at least, when he was still far from Naples.   Thus a

repetition of the Sicilian dictatorship would be impossible. To what measures he resorted is not known with any accuracy; he was carrying on a policy without the knowledge of the king or the cabinet, and no trustworthy account exists of it. What is known is that Cavour, as a conspirator, failed.

Till the Captain of the Thousand appeared, the people would not move. They knew nothing of the merits of a limited monarchy, but they could vibrate to the electric thrill of a great emotion, such as that which made their hearts rise and swell when the organ in the village church pealed forth the airs of Bellini or Donizetti on a feast day. Garibaldi was the Mahdi of a new dispensation, which was to end earthquakes, the cholera, poverty, to heal all wounds, dry all tears. Yes, it was worth while to rise now! King Francis seems to have understood the situation; he sat down to wait for Destiny in a red shirt. When the liberator was sufficiently near, he is reported to have called the commanders of the National Guard, and to have addressed them in these words: "As your—that is, our common friend, Don Peppe, approaches, my work ends and yours begins. Keep the peace. I have ordered the troops that remain to capitulate."

The British Government had all along recommended Cavour to leave Garibaldi alone to finish the task he had so well begun; he did not take the advice, but in the end he must have recognised its wisdom. At the very last moment it might have been possible to get Victor Emmanuel's authority proclaimed at Naples before Garibaldi entered the city, or, at any rate, Cavour thought so; but the attempt would have worn a graceless look at that late hour, and it was not made. Cavour never forgot the services which Garibaldi had rendered to Italy; "the greatest," he said, "that a man could render her." When the dissension between them began, he might have convoked Parliament and fought out the battle before the Chamber, but, though he would have saved his *prestige*, he would have lost Italy. He preferred to risk his reputation and to save Italy. In order to make Italy, he believed it to be of vital importance to keep the hero on good terms with the king. Garibaldi was a great moral power, not only in Italy, but in Europe. If Cavour entered into a struggle with him, he would have the majority of old diplomatists on his side, but European public opinion would be against him, and it would be right. He argued thus with those who mistook his forbearance for weakness, when it was really strength.

Cavour seriously thought that among the inconvenient consequences of Garibaldi's ascendency might be a war with Austria, forced on the Government by the victorious *condottiere* in the intoxication of success. He was resolved as a statesman to do what he could to prevent so great an imprudence. He had assured the British Government in writing that he had no present intention of attacking Austria, and in this he was perfectly sincere. Still he did not shrink from the possibility. He wrote to Ricasoli: "If we were beaten by overwhelming force, the cause of Italy would not be lost; she would arise from her ruins, as Piedmont arose from the field of Novara." To another friend he made what was, perhaps, the only boast he ever uttered: "I would answer for the result if I possessed the art of war as I possess the art of politics." For the rest, he added characteristically, When a course became the only one, what was the good of counting up its dangers? You ought to find out the way of overcoming them.

CHAPTER XII

THE KINGDOM OF ITALY

WHEN Garibaldi entered Naples, Cavour had already decided on the momentous step of sending the king's forces into Umbria and the Marches of Ancona. At the end of August he wrote: "We are touching the supreme moment; with God's help, Italy will be made in three months." If constitutional monarchy was to triumph it could no longer stand still; neither Austrian arms nor republican propaganda could so jeopardise the scheme of an Italian kingdom under a prince of the House of Savoy as the demonstration of facts that the Government of Victor Emmanuel had lost the lead. Moreover, it became daily more probable that, if the king did not invade the Roman States from the north, Garibaldi would invade them from the south, and this Cavour was determined to prevent. If a Garibaldian invasion succeeded, France would come into the field; if it failed, all the great results hitherto accomplished would be compromised. Garibaldi at most could only have disposed of half his little army of volunteers, and in Lamoricière, the conqueror of Abd-el-Kader, he would have met a stouter antagonist than the Bourbon generals.

But the party of action urged him towards Rome, cost what it might, with the impracticability of men who expect the walls of cities to fall at the blast of the trumpet. Every reason, patriotic, political, geographical, justified Cavour's resolution. It was only by force that Umbria and the Marches had been retained under the papal sway in 1859 ; there was not an Italian who did not look on their liberation as a patriotic duty. The nominal pretext for the war, as has happened in most of the wars of this century, only partially touched the point at issue ; Cavour professed to see a menace in the increase of the Pope's army, and demanded its disbandment. In a literal sense, fifteen or twenty thousand men could not be a menace to Italy. Still it must be doubted if any state could have tolerated, in what was now its midst, even this small force, commanded by a foreign general, composed largely of foreign recruits, and proclaiming itself the advance guard of reactionary Europe. Lamoricière said that wherever the revolution appeared, it must be knocked on the head as if it were a mad dog. By "the revolution" he meant Italian unity.

Cavour, the cabinet, and the king were already labouring under the penalties of excommunication by the Bull issued in the spring against all who had taken part in the annexation of Romagna. When Prince Charles of Lorraine in 1690 advised the Emperor to withdraw his claims to Spain and concentrate his energies on uniting Italy, he observed that in order to join the kingdom of Naples with Lombardy, it would be necessary to reduce the Pope to the sole city of Rome. This most able statesman of the House of Hapsburg continued : " The services of very learned doctors should be obtained to instruct the people, both by word of mouth and by writing, on the inutility and illusion of excommunications when it is a question of temporalities, which Jesus Christ never destined to His Church, and which she cannot possess without outraging His example and compromising His Gospel." Cavour did not seek the learned doctors, because he knew that the religious side of the matter, however vital it seemed to the young Breton noblemen who enlisted under Lamoricière, left unmoved the Pope's subjects, who had a mixture of scorn and hatred for the rule of priests, such as was not felt for any government in Italy. For the rest, familiarity lessens the effect of spiritual fulminations, and even of those not spiritual. For three months Cavour had sustained the running fire of all except one of the foreign representatives at Turin; as he wrote to the Marquis E. d'Azeglio: "I have the whole *corps diplomatique* on my back, Hudson excepted; I let them have their say and I go on." He deplored the sad fate of diplomacy, which always took the most interest in bad causes, and was the more favourable to a government the worse it was.[1] If *ces messieurs* protested or departed, they must; he could not arrest the current. If he tried, it would carry him away with it, "which would not be a great evil," but it would carry away the dynasty also. The Peace of Villafranca had caused the Italians to conceive an irresistible desire for unity—events were stronger than men, and he should only stop before fleets and armies.

It appears that this time Cavour would have acted

[1] We are reminded of a remark of Prince Bismarck: "Personne, pas même le plus malveillant démocrate, ne se fait une idée de ce qu'il y a de nullité et de charlatanisme dans cette diplomatie."

even without the assent of Napoleon ; it was, however, evidently of great moment to secure it if possible.   The Emperor was making a tour in the newly acquired province of Savoy when General Cialdini and L. C. Farini were despatched by Cavour to endeavour to win him over.   The interview, which was held at Chambéry, was kept so secret that its precise date is not now known.   Cavour tried, not for the first time, the effect of entire frankness.   He counted on persuading Napoleon that their interests were identical : the White Reaction and the Red Republic were the enemies of both.   He did not neglect the item that Lamoricière was disliked at the Tuileries.   With regard to Garibaldi, he represented that since the cession of Nice no one could manage him.   The end of it was that, if Napoleon did not say the words "Faites, mais faites vite," which rumour attributed to him, he certainly expressed their substance.

On September 11 the Sardinian army, more than double as strong as Lamoricière's, crossed the papal frontier.   With the exception of England and Sweden, all the Powers recalled their representatives from Turin. The French Ministry telegraphed to Napoleon, who was at Marseilles, to ask what they were to do.   They got no answer, and, left to their own inspiration, they informed the Duke de Grammont, the French Ambassador at Rome, that the Emperor's Government "would not tolerate" the culpable aggression of Sardinia, and that orders were given to embark troops for Ancona.   These misleading assurances encouraged Lamoricière, but in any case he would probably have thought it incumbent on him to make what stand he could.   He was defeated by Cialdini on the heights of Castelfidardo—"yesterday unknown, to-day immortal," as Mgr. Dupanloup eloquently exclaimed. Ancona fell to a combined attack from land and sea. Meanwhile Fanti advanced on Perugia, and was on the point of entering Viterbo when a detachment from the French garrison in Rome suddenly occupied the town : one of Napoleon's facing-both-ways evolutions by which he thought to save the goat and cabbages of the Italian riddle, but the final result was to lose both one and the other. Lamoricière went home, declaring that he took his defeat less to heart than the cruel disillusions he had undergone in Rome. Some one proposed that he should go to the rescue of King Francis, but he answered that his wish had been to serve the Pope, not the Neapolitan Bourbons.

On the 20th the King of Sardinia, at the head of his army, marched into the kingdom of Naples. For the Continental Powers it was a new act of aggression ; for Lord Palmerston, a measure of the highest expediency, to which he had been urging Cavour with an impatience hardly exceeded by that of the most ardent Italian patriot. The goal of Italian unity was now more than in sight—it was touched. The Rubicon was crossed in more senses than one. But at this last stage there arose a danger which Cavour had not seriously apprehended. He thought that Austria would not attack, unless directly provoked by some imprudence of the extreme party. She had allowed the Grand Duke of Tuscany and the King of Naples to fall; why should she be more concerned for the Pope ? Austria's concern for the Pope was, in fact, not very deep, but there were Austrian politicians who argued that, if Venetia was to be saved for the empire, the right of Austria to hold it

must rest on something more solid than a treaty, every
other clause of which had been torn to shreds. Never
could a time return so favourable as the present for
striking a blow at the nascent Italian kingdom. With the
king and the best part of the army in the south, who
was there to oppose them? It is true that there was a
feeling, growing and expanding silently, which tended
all the other way : a feeling that enough of German and
Hungarian and Bohemian and Polish blood had been
poured out upon Italian plains; that there was a fate
in the thing, and the fate was contrary to Austria. This
feeling grew and grew till the day when Venice too was
lost, and not a man in Austria could find it in his heart
to cast one sincere look of regret behind at all that
fabric of splendid but ill-fortune-bringing dominion. A
few years were still to pass, however, before that day
came, and all the forces of the old order combined to
press the Emperor to oppose the invading flood while
there was time. Some say that he had actually signed
the order to cross the frontier, but that on second
thoughts he decided first to seek the co-operation of
Russia, probably with a view to keeping France quiet.
When he went to Warsaw in October, he left everything
prepared for war on his return. But Alexander II.,
having thrown overboard his old friends at Naples, did
not want to help the Pope. The Emperor of Austria
was badly received by the people of Warsaw, and this
tended against the alliance. The Prince Regent of
Prussia, who travelled to Warsaw to meet him, definitely
refused to guarantee his Venetian possessions. Lord
John Russell had lately met the Prussian ruler and his
minister, Schleinitz, at Coblentz, and had used all his

influence to persuade them to keep Germany out of Italian concerns. Though the Berlin Government loudly protested against the Sardinian attack on papal territory, there is no doubt that the voice of Prussia at Warsaw was raised in favour of peace.

At this juncture Napoleon proposed the usual Congress. While he told Cavour that he must not expect assistance from him, his private language towards the Northern Powers did not exclude the possibility of French intervention. A diversion was created by a note which Lord John Russell addressed to Sir James Hudson, "the most unprincipled document," as it was called at Rome, "that had ever been written by the minister of any civilised court." Lord John defended every act of Sardinia in the strongest and plainest terms, and people grew almost more angry with him than with Cavour. The Italian statesman never quailed through this last perilous crisis; "Nous sommes prêts," he wrote, "à jouer le tout pour le tout." There are moments when the problems of politics, as of life, cease to perplex. By degrees the storm-clouds rolled away without breaking. In November Cavour felt himself strong enough to affirm that the questions of Naples and the Marches were purely Italian, and that the Powers of Europe had no business to meddle with them. During the autumn, amidst other cares, he was seriously preoccupied by a persistent rumour that his faithful friend, Sir James Hudson, was to be removed to make room for the ex-British Minister at Naples, whose occupation was gone through the fall of the dynasty. It has been denied that the change was then contemplated; at any rate it was not carried out till a later period, and Cavour had the comfort of keeping his English fellow-worker near him till he died.

The Garibaldian epic closed with the battle near the left bank of the Volturno on October 1. Still Garibaldi showed no disposition to resign the dictatorship, or to abandon the designs on Rome which he had postponed, not renounced. On his side, Cavour was resolved that a normal government should be established at Naples, and that Garibaldi should not go to Rome, but he was no less resolved that, as far as he could compass it, the giver of two crowns should be generously treated. Unfortunately Fanti, the virtual head of the royal army, represented the old military prejudice which classed volunteers with banditti. A violent scene took place between this general and Cavour; Fanti wished that the Garibaldians should be simply sent home with a gratuity, alleging that "the exigencies of the army" were opposed to the recognition of their grades. Cavour replied that they were not in Spain,—in Italy the army obeyed. The ministerial emissaries in the south received instructions (which they did not invariably execute) to spare no pains to act in harmony with the dictator. Cavour, himself, treated him always as a power and an equal. He took care that he was the first to whom the secret of the invasion of the Marches was confided. He assured him that in case of a war with Austria he would be called upon to play an important part. When the king started on the march for Naples, Cavour wrote to him advising that "infinite regard" should be paid to the leader of the Thousand; "Garibaldi," he added, "has become my most violent enemy, but I desire for the good of Italy, and the honour of your Majesty, that he should retire entirely satisfied." To L. C. Farini, who accompanied the king to Naples, he wrote that the whole of Europe would condemn them if they sacrificed to military pedantry men who had given their blood for Italy. He would bury himself at Leri for the rest of his life rather than be responsible for an act of such black ingratitude. In spite of all he could do, however, a certain grudging spirit hung about the conduct of Piedmontese officialdom towards the volunteers and their chief, but great personal offers were made to Garibaldi—the highest military rank, a castle, a ship, the dowry of a princess for his daughter. All was refused. Garibaldi asked for the governorship of the Two Sicilies for a year with unlimited power, and this, in the opinion of every person of weight in Italy, it was impossible to grant.

In reviewing Cavour's conduct of affairs at this point, it is important to dwell on his unwavering fidelity to constitutional methods. We know now that he was strongly urged to take an opposite course. Ricasoli telegraphed to him : " The master stroke would be to proclaim the dictatorship of the king." The Iron Baron told Victor Emmanuel to his face that it was humiliating for him to accept half Italy as the gift even of a hero. It was no time for scruples ; the *coup d'état* would be legitimised afterwards by universal suffrage ; Garibaldi himself would approve of the king's dictatorship if it were accompanied by a thoroughly Italian policy. This was perfectly true ; as Cavour said, the conception was really the same as Garibaldi's own : a great revolutionary dictatorship to be exercised in the name of the king without the control of a free press, and with no

individual or parliamentary guarantees.   But Cavour
would have none of it.   What, he asked, would England
say to a *coup d'état?*   His hope had always been that
Italy might make herself a nation without passing
through the hands of a Cromwell; that she might win
independence without sacrificing liberty, and abolish
monarchical absolutism without falling into revolutionary
despotism.   From parliament alone could be drawn the
moral force capable of subduing factions.

Not from his fellow-countrymen only, but from some
who believed themselves to be Italy's best friends
abroad, came the prompting of the tempter: more power!
Few ministers in a predicament of such vast difficulty
would have resisted the evil fascination of those two
words.   Cavour heard them unmoved.   He told his
various counsellors that they counted too much on his
influence, and were too distrustful of liberty.   He had
no confidence in dictatorships, least of all in civil
dictatorships; with a parliament many things could be
done which would be impossible to absolute power.
The experience of thirteen years convinced him that an
honest and energetic ministry, which had nothing to
fear from the revelations of the tribune, and which was
not of a humour to be intimidated by extreme parties,
gained far more than it lost by parliamentary struggles.
He never felt so weak as when the Chambers were
closed.   In a letter to Mme. de Circourt, he said that, if
people succeeded in persuading the Italians that they
needed a dictator, they would choose Garibaldi, not
himself, and they would be right.   He summed up the
matter thus: "I cannot betray my origin, deny the
principles of all my life.   I am the son of liberty, and to

it I owe all that I am. If a veil is to be placed on its statue, it is not for me to do it."

Meanwhile the edge of the precipice was reached. The king was marching on, and still the dictator held the post which he owed to his sword and the popular will. He openly begged the king to dismiss his minister (in his idea kings could change their ministers as easily as dictators). The public challenge could not be ignored. There was no time to lose, and Cavour lost none ; his answer was an appeal to parliament. "A man," he said, "whom the country holds justly dear has stated that he has no confidence in us. It behoves parliament to declare whether we shall retire or continue our work." He invited the deputies to pass a Bill authorising the king's Government to accept the immediate annexation of such provinces of Central and Southern Italy as manifested by universal suffrage their desire to become an integral part of the constitutional monarchy of Victor Emmanuel. This was voted on October 11. The majority of Cavour's party did not believe that Garibaldi would give in to the national mandate ; he knew him better. On the 13th the dictator called together his advisers of all shades of opinion. There was a heated discussion : a solution seemed farther off than ever. Then, when they had all spoken, the chief rose serenely and said that, if annexation were the will of the people, he would have annexation; *si faccia l' Italia !* He decreed the plebiscite, but, having made up his mind, he did not wait for its verdict. He issued one more ukase : "that the Two Sicilies form an integral part of Italy, one and indivisible under the constitutional king, Victor Emmanuel, and his successors." By a stroke of the pen he handed over his conquests as a free gift. It was not constitutional, still less democratic ; puritan republicans averted their eyes, so did rigid monarchists, but Cavour was perfectly content. He had forced Garibaldi's hand without straining the royal prerogative or the minister's authority. He had gained his end, and he had not betrayed freedom. It could be argued now with more force than in 1860 that Garibaldi and Ricasoli were right in contending that the best government for the southern populations, only just released from a demoralising yoke, would have been a wise, temporary despotism. But despotisms have the habit of being neither wise nor temporary, and, apart from this, the establishment of any partial or regional rule, which placed the south under different institutions from the rest of Italy, would have killed Italian Unity at its birth.

Cavour went on a brief visit to Naples, his name having been the first to be drawn when the deputies were chosen who were to take the congratulations of parliament to the king. Umbria, the Marches, and the kingdoms of Sicily and Naples were joined to the common family. Much had, indeed, been done, but there was trouble still at Gaeta, where Napoleon placed his fleet in such a position as to render an attack from the sea impossible. It was difficult to decide if dust-throwing were the object, or if Napoleonic ideas had taken a new turn. Italy was made, but it might be unmade. This was what French politicians were constantly repeating. "L'Italie est une invention de l'Empereur," said M. Rouher. "Rome l'engloutira !" predicted M. de Girardin. Italy, declared M. Thiers, was an historical parasite which lived on its past and

could have no future. If all this were so, the waters
would be disturbed again soon, and there might be play
for anglers. The Murat scheme would have a new
chance, were Victor Emmanuel tried and found wanting.
Young Prince Murat confided to his friends that he
expected to be wanted soon at Naples; "a great bore,"
but he would do his duty and go if required.

Whatever purpose Napoleon had in view, he was
induced, at last, by the British Government to desist
from prolonging a struggle which could only end in one
way. The French fleet was withdrawn in January
1861, and Gaeta capitulated on February 13. King
Francis began the sad life of exile, which closed a few
years ago at Arco. The true Bourbon takes misfortune
easily; the pleasures of a mock court are dear to him,
his spirits never fail, nor does his appetite. But
Francis II., the son of a Savoyard mother, never con-
soled himself for the loss of country and crown.

Cavour hoped that with the fall of Gaeta the state of
the old *Regno* would rapidly improve, but another
citadel remained to the reaction—Rome, whence the
campaign against unity continued to be directed. A
veritable *terreur blanche*, called by one side brigandage,
by the other a holy war, possessed the hills from
Vesuvius to the Sila forest. But though there were
several foreign noblemen who took part in it, not one
Neapolitan of respectability or standing joined the
insurgents. The general elections showed in the south,
as over the whole country, a large majority pledged to
support Cavour. The first act of the new Chamber was to
vote the assumption of the title of King of Italy by Victor
Emmanuel. The king might have assumed the title a

year before with more correctness than the Longobard kings of Italy or the First Consul, but he did well to wait till none could gainsay his right to it. Some faddists proposed to substitute "King of the Italians." Cavour replied that the title of King of Italy was the consecration of a great fact : the transformation of the country, whose very existence as a nation was denied, into the kingdom of Italy. It condensed into one word the history of the work achieved. On the proclamation of the new kingdom Cavour resigned office; Victor Emmanuel, who was never really at his ease with Cavour, thought of accepting in earnest what was done as a matter of form, but Ricasoli dissuaded him from the idea. The Cavour ministry therefore returned to office, with a few modifications.

The new Chamber represented all Italy, except Rome and Venice. From Villafranca to his death, Venice was never out of Cavour's mind. He kept in touch with the revolutionary forces in Hungary, and Kossuth believed to the last that, if Cavour had lived, he would have compassed the liberation of both Hungary and Venetia within the year 1862. He would have supported Lord John Russell's plan, which was that Italy should buy the Herzegovina and give it to Austria in exchange for Venetia, but, on the whole, he thought that the most likely solution was war, in which Prussia and Italy were ranged on the same side. He, almost alone, rated at its true value the latent military force of Prussia. He had a knack of calling Prussia "Germany," as he used to call Piedmont "Italy." He turned off the furious remonstrances which came like the burden of a song from Berlin, with the polite remark that the Prussian

Government would be soon very glad to follow his example. When William I. ascended the throne, he ignored the rupture of diplomatic relations, and sent La Marmora to whisper into the ear of the new monarch words of artful flattery. He may have doubted if a Prussianised Germany would exactly come as a boon and a blessing to men. In 1848 he prophesied that Germanism would disturb the European equilibrium, and that the future German Empire would aim at becoming a naval power in order to combat and rival England on the seas. But he saw that the rise of Prussia meant the decline of Austria, and this was all that, as an Italian statesman, with Venetia still in chains, he was bound to consider.

CHAPTER XIII

ROME VOTED THE CAPITAL—CONCLUSION

THE other unsolved question, that of Rome, was the most thorny, the most complicated, that ever a statesman had to grapple with. Though Cavour's death makes it impossible to say what measure of success would have attended his plans for resolving it, it must be always interesting to study his attitude in approaching the greatest crux in modern politics.

Cavour did not think of shirking this question because it was difficult. In fact, he had understood from the beginning that in it lay the essence of the whole problem. Chiefly for that reason he brought the occupations of the Papal States before the Congress of Paris. In 1856, as in 1861, he looked upon the Temporal Power as incompatible with the independence of Italy. It was already a fiction. "The Pope's domination as sovereign ceased from the day when it was proved that it could not exist save by a double foreign occupation." It had become a centre of corruption, which destroyed moral sense and rendered religious sentiment null. Without the Temporal Power, many of the wounds of the Church might be healed. It was

useless to cite the old argument of the independence of
the head of the Church ; in face of a double occupation
and the Swiss troops, it would be too bitter a mockery.
When Cavour spoke in these terms, Italian Unity
seemed far off. Now that it was accomplished, a new
and potent motive arose for settling the Roman question
once for all. In May 1861 Mr. Disraeli remarked to
Count Vitzthum : "The sooner the inevitable war breaks
out the better. The Italian card-house can never last.
Without Rome there is no Italy. But that the French
will evacuate the Eternal City is highly improbable.
On this point the interests of the Conservative party
coincide with those of Napoleon." There is no better
judge of the drift of political affairs than an out-and-out
opponent. So Prince Metternich always insisted that
the Italians did not want reforms—they wanted national
existence, unity. Mr. Disraeli probably had in mind a
speech delivered in the House of Commons by Lord
John Russell, in which the Foreign Secretary recommended as "the best arrangement" the Pope's retention
of Rome with a small surrounding territory. There is
no doubt that a large part of the moderate party in
Italy would have then endorsed this recommendation.
They looked upon *Roma capitale* as what D' Azeglio called
it—a classical fantasticality. What was the good of
making an old man uncomfortable, upsetting the religious
susceptibilities of Europe, forfeiting the complaisance of
France, in order to pitch the tent of the nation in a
malarious town which was only fit to be a museum?
Those who only partly comprehended Cavour's character
might have expected to find him favourable to these
opinions, which had a certain specious appearance of

practical good sense. But Cavour saw through the husk to the kernel; he saw that "without Rome there was no Italy."

Without Rome Italian Unity was still only a name. Rome was the symbol, as it was the safeguard of unity. Without it, Italy would remain a conglomeration of provinces, a union, not a unit—not the great nation which Cavour had laboured to create. Even as prime minister of little Piedmont, he had spurned a parochial policy. He had no notion of a humble, semi-neutralised Italy, which should have no voice in the world. Cavour lacked the sense of poetry, of art; he hated fads, and he did not believe in the perfectibility of the human species, but his prose was the prose of the ancient Roman; it was the prose of empire. United Italy must be a great power or nothing. Cavour was practical and prudent, as he is represented in the portrait commonly drawn of him, but there was a larger side to his character, which has been less often discerned. Nor is it to be con- jectured that the direction Italy has taken, and the consequent outlay in armaments and ships, would have been blamed by him, though he would have blamed the uncontrolled waste of money in all departments, which is answerable for the present state of the finances. Nor, again, would Cavour have disapproved of colonial enter- prises, but he would have taken care to have the meat, not the bones: Tunis, not Massowah. From the opening to the close of his career, the thought "I am an Italian citizen" governed all his acts. Those who accused him of provincialism, of regionalism, mistook the tastes of the private individual for the convictions of the states- man. He preferred the flats and fogs of Leri to the scenery of the Bay of Naples; but in politics he did not acquire the feelings of an Italian: he was born with them. It has been said that he aggrandised Piedmont; it would be truer to say that he sacrificed it. For years he drained its resources; he sent its soldiers to die in the Crimea; he exposed it again and again to the risk of invasion; he tore from it two of its fairest provinces. But there was one thing that he would not do; he would not dethrone Turin to begin a new "regionalism" elsewhere. At Rome alone the history of the Italian municipalities would become the history of the Italian nation.

Cavour deliberately departed from his usual rule of letting events shape themselves when he pledged himself and the monarchy to the policy of making Rome the capital. In October 1860 he said from his place in parliament that it was a grave thing for a minister to pronounce his opinion on the great questions of the future, but a statesman worthy of the name ought to have certain fixed points by which he steered his course. For twelve years their continual object had been national independence; henceforth it was "to make the Eternal City, on which rested twenty-five centuries of glory, the splendid capital of the Italian kingdom."

On March 25, 1861, Cavour seized a chance opportunity to repeat and emphasise his views. The question of Rome was, he said, the gravest ever placed before the parliament of a free people. It was not only of vital importance to Italy, but also to two hundred million Catholics in all parts of the globe; its solution ought to have not only a political influence, but also a moral and religious influence. In the previous year he had deemed it wise to speak with reserve, but now that this question was the principal subject of discussion in all civilised nations, reserve would not be prudence but pusillanimity. He proceeded to lay down as an irrefragable fact that Rome must become the capital of Italy. Only this could end the discords and differences of the various parts of the country. The position of the capital was not decided by reasons of climate or topography, or even of strategy. The choice of the capital was determined by great moral reasons, by the voice of national senti-ment. Cavour rarely introduced his own personality even into his private letters, much less into his speeches; for the last ten years of his life he seemed a living policy, hardly a man. But in this speech there is a touch of personal pathos in the passage in which he said that, for himself, it would be a grievous day when he had to leave his native Turin with its straight, formal streets, for Rome and its splendid monuments, for which he was not artist enough to care. He called upon the future Italy, established firmly in the Eternal City, to remember the cradle of her liberties, which had made such great sacrifices for her, and was ready to make this one too !

They must go to Rome, he continued, but on two conditions—the first was, concert with France; the second, that the union of this city with Italy should not be interpreted by the great mass of Catholics as the signal for the servitude of the Church. They must go to Rome without lessening the Pope's real independence, and without extending the power of the civil authority over the spiritual. History proved that the union of civil and spiritual authority in the same hands was fatal

to progress and freedom.   The possession of Rome by
Italy must put an end to this union, not begin a new
phase of it by making the Pope a sort of head chaplain
or chief almoner to the Italian state.   The Pope's
spiritual authority would be safer in the charge of
twenty-six millions of free Italians than in that of a
foreign garrison.   Whether they went to Rome with or
without the consent of the Pontiff, as soon as the fall
of the Temporal Power was proclaimed, the complete
liberty of the Church would be proclaimed also.   Might
they not hope that the head of the Church would accept
the offered terms ?   Was it impossible to persuade him
that the Temporal Power was no longer a guarantee of
independence, and that its loss would be compensated
by an amount of liberty which the Church had sought
in vain for three centuries, only gathering particles of it
by concordats which conceded the use of spiritual arms
to temporal rulers ?   They were ready to promise the
Holy Father that freedom which he had never obtained
from those who called themselves his allies and devoted
sons.   They were ready to assert through every portion
of the king's dominions the great principle of *a free
church in a free state*.

At Cavour's invitation, parliament voted the choice
of Rome as capital.   From that vote there could be no
going back.   *Roma capitale* could never again be put
aside as the dream of revolutionists and poets.   This
was the last great political act of Cavour's life.   Though
he did not think that his life would be a long one, he
thought that he should have time to finish his work
himself.   One day, when he had been discussing the
matter with a friend, who saw nothing but difficulties,

he placed the inkstand at the top of the table before which they were sitting, and said, "I see the straight line to that point; it is this" (he traced it with his finger). "Supposing that halfway I encounter an impediment; I do not knock my head against it for the pleasure of breaking it, but neither do I go back. I look to the right and to the left, and not being able to follow the straight line, I make a curve. I turn the obstacle which I cannot attack in front."

What Cavour would have called the straight line to Rome was a friendly arrangement with the Pope. He could not have hoped for this, had he been less convinced that the true interests of the Church of Rome would be served, not injured, by the loss of a sovereignty which had become an anachronism. It is, of course, certain that many thought the contrary; Lord Palmerston believed that the religious position of the papacy would suffer, and among the advanced party the wish to weaken the spiritual influence of the priests went along with the wish to abolish their political dominion. Cavour looked upon religion as a great moralising force, and he was well assured that the only form of it acceptable to the Italian people was the Latin form of Christianity established in Rome. Efforts to spread Protestantism in Italy struck him as childish. Freed from the log of temporalities, he expected that the Church would become constantly better fitted to perform its mission.

Cavour began negotiations with Rome which, at first, he had reason to think, were favourably entertained; afterwards they were abruptly broken off. Nothing is more difficult than to penetrate through the wall of

P

apparent unanimity which surrounds the Vatican. Sometimes, however, a breach is made, to the scandal of the
faithful. Thus the biographer of Cardinal Manning
revealed the fact that the late Archbishop of West-
minster, who began by wishing the Temporal Power to
be erected into an article of faith, ended by ardently
desiring some kind of tacitly accepted *modus vivendi* with
the Italian kingdom, such as that which Cavour proposed.
Cardinal Manning was sorry to see the Italians being
driven to atheism and socialism, and so he had the
courage to change his mind. In 1861 he was 'in the
opposite camp, but there was not wanting then a section
of learned and patriotic ecclesiastics who desired peace.
It was said that their efforts were rendered sterile by
the great organisation which a pope once suppressed,
and which owed its resurrection to a schismatic emperor
and an heretical king. However that may be, the
recollection of what befell Clement XIV. is still a living
force in Rome.

Having failed to conclude a compact with the Vatican,
Cavour turned to France. To make it easier for
Napoleon to withdraw his troops, he was willing to
allow the Temporal Power to stand for a short time—"for
instance, for a year"—after their departure. In the
arrangement subsequently arrived at under the name of
the September Convention, the underlying intention was
to adjourn *Roma capitale* to the Greek kalends. Cavour
had no such intention, nor would he have agreed to the
transference of the capital to Florence. His plan was
warmly supported by Prince Napoleon, and had he lived
it is probable that it would have been carried out. He
did not despair of an ultimate reconciliation with the

Holy See, though he no longer thought that it would yield to persuasion alone.

While Cavour was applying himself with feverish activity to the Roman question, he was harassed by the state of the Neapolitan provinces, which showed no improvement. The liquidation of Garibaldi's dictatorship was rendered the more difficult by the undiminished dislike of the military chiefs for the volunteers, whom they were disposed to treat less favourably than the Bourbon officers who ran away. Cavour hoped to get substantial justice done in the end, but meantime he had to bear the blame for the illiberality which he had so strenuously opposed. To have told the truth would have been to throw discredit on the army, and this he would not do. The subject was brought before the Chamber of Deputies in a debate opened by Ricasoli, who spoke in favour of the volunteers, but deprecated undue importance being assigned to the work of any private citizen. The true liberator of Italy was the king under whom they had all worked; those whose sphere of action had been widest, as their utility had been greatest, should feel thankful for so precious a privilege—few men could say, "I have served my country well, I have entirely done my duty." Cavour, who heard Ricasoli speak for the first time, said with generous approbation, "I have understood to-day what real eloquence is." But it was not likely that the debate would continue on this academic plane. Garibaldi had come to Turin in a fit of intense anger at the treatment of his old comrades, and on rising to defend them he soon lost control over himself, and launched into furious invectives against the man who had made him a foreigner in his native town, and "who was now driving the country into civil war." Cavour would have borne patiently anything that Garibaldi could say about Nice, but at the words "civil war" he became violently excited. The house trembled lest a scene should take place, which would be worse for Italy than the loss of a battle. But Cavour cared too much for Italy to harm her. The sense of his first indignant protests was lost in the general uproar; afterwards, when he rose to reply to Garibaldi, he was perfectly calm; there was not a trace of resentment on his face. Such self-command would have been noble in a man whose temperament was phlegmatic; in a passionate man like Cavour it was heroic. He said that an abyss had been created between himself and General Garibaldi. He had performed what he believed to be a duty, but it was the most cruel duty of his life. What he felt made him able to understand what Garibaldi felt. With regard to the volunteers, had he not himself instituted them in 1859 in the teeth of all kinds of opposition? Was it likely that he wished to treat them ill? A few days later Garibaldi wrote a letter in which he promised Cavour (in effect) plenary absolution if he would proclaim a dictatorship. He would then be the first to obey. There was no petty spite or envy in Garibaldi; his wild thrusts had been prompted by "a general honest thought, and common good to all." He was ready to give his rival unlimited power.

By the king's wish, Cavour and Garibaldi met and exchanged a few courteous, if not cordial, words. Cavour ignored the scene in the Chamber; he had already said that for him it had never happened. It was their last meeting. The wear and tear of public life as it was lived by Cavour must have been enormous; it meant the concentration, not only of the mental and physical powers, but also of the nervous and emotional faculties, on a single object. He had not the relaxation of athletic or literary tastes, or the repose of a cheerful domestic life. Latterly he even gave up going to the theatre in order to dose undisturbed. A doctor warned him not to work after dinner, and to take frequent holidays in the mountains; he neglected both rules. He was inclined to despise rest. He used to say: "When I want a thing to be done quickly, I always go to a busy man: the unoccupied man never has any time." He, himself, did not know how to be idle; yet he was painfully conscious of overwork and brain-fag. He told his friend Castelli that he was tormented by sleeplessness, but still more by certain ideas which assailed him at night, and which he could not get rid of. He got up and walked about the room, but all was useless; "I am no longer master of my head." When Parliament was open, he never missed a sitting, and he left nothing to subordinates in the several departments in his charge. While his mental processes remained clear and orderly, the brain, when not governed by the will, did its tasks as a tired slave does them; thus he was surrounded by a mass of confused papers and documents, amongst which he sometimes had to seek for days for the one required at the moment.

In the last half of May he was noticed to be unwontedly irritable and impatient of contradiction. The debates bored him; on the last day that he sat in his accustomed place, he said that, when Italy was made,

he would bring in a Bill to abolish all the chairs of
rhetoric. That evening he was taken ill with fever;
his own physician was absent, and he dictated a treatment to the doctor who was called in, which he thought
would make his illness a short one. He was bled five
times in four days. On the fourth day he summoned a
cabinet council to his bedside; the ministers, sharing his
own opinion that he was better, allowed it to be pro-
longed for several hours. When they went out, an old
friend came in and read death in his face. Other
doctors were consulted, and the treatment was changed.
It was too late. From the first the chance of recovery
was small, owing to the mental tension at which Cavour
had lived for months; whatever chance there was had
been thrown away. He knew people when he first saw
them, but then fell back into lethargy or delirium.
Suddenly he said: "The king must be told."

When the case became evidently desperate, the
family sent for a monk, named Fra Giacomo, who had
promised Cavour during the cholera epidemic of 1854
that the refusal of the sacraments to Santa Rosa should
not be repeated in his own extremity. An excited
crowd gathered round the palace. One workman said:
"If the priests refuse, a word and we will finish them
all." But Fra Giàcomo kept his promise. "I know the
Count," he said (for many years he had dispensed his
private charities); "a clasp of the hand will be
sufficient." On the evening of the same day, June 5,
the king ascended the secret staircase leading to Cavour's
bedroom, which had been so often mounted before dawn
by too compromising visitors. Cavour exclaimed on
seeing him: "O Maestà!" but the recognition seemed

not to last. "These Neapolitans, they must be cleansed," he said, interrupting the sovereign's kind commonplaces of a hope that was not. Then he ordered that his secretary, Artom, should be ready to transact business with him at five next morning; "there was no time to lose." Cavour's biographers have repeated statements as to precepts and injunctions spoken by him in his last hours. But he was continually delirious; all that could be understood was that his wandering mind was running on what had been the life of his life, Italy. In the early dawn of the 6th, he imagined that he was making a ministerial statement from his place in the Chamber of Deputies; his voice sounded clear and distinct, but ideas, names, words, were incoherently mixed together. At four o'clock he became silent, and very soon life was pronounced to be extinct.

One Sunday in June, a year before, Cavour spent some hours in the ancestral castle at Santena, which he so rarely visited. On that occasion he said to the village syndic: "Here I wish my bones to rest." The wish was respected, the king yielding to it his own desire to give his great minister a royal burial at the Superga. Cavour had the old sentiment that it was well for a man to be buried where his fathers were buried, and to die in their faith. At all times it would have been repugnant to him to pose as a sceptic, most of all on his deathbed. Once, when he was reminded in the Campo Santo at Pisa that he was standing on holy earth brought from Palestine, he said, smiling, "Perhaps they will make a saint of me some day." He died a Catholic, and, instead of launching its censures against Fra Giacomo, the Church might have written "ancor questo" among its triumphs.

For the rest, with minds such as Cavour's, religion is not the mystical elevation of the soul towards God, but the intellectual assent to the ruling of a superior will, and religious forms are, in substance, symbols of that assent. The essence of Cavour's theology and morality is expressed in two sayings of Epictetus. One is, that as to piety to the gods, the chief thing is to have right opinions about them; to think that they exist, and that they administer the all well and justly. The other is: For this is your duty, to act well the part that is given to you.

"Cavour," said Lord Palmerston in the classic home of constitutional liberty, the British House of Commons, "left a name 'to point a moral and adorn a tale.'" The moral was, that a man of transcendent talent, indomitable industry, inextinguishable patriotism, could overcome difficulties which seemed insurmountable, and confer the greatest, the most inestimable benefits on his country. The tale with which his memory would be associated was the most extraordinary, the most romantic, in the annals of the world. A people which seemed dead had arisen to new and vigorous life, breaking the spell which bound it, and showing itself worthy of a new and splendid destiny. The man whose name would go down to posterity linked with such events might have died too soon for the hopes of his fellow-citizens, not for his fame and his glory.

After thirty-seven years nothing need be taken away from this high eulogy, and something can be added. The completion of the national edifice within a decade of Cavour's death was still, in a sense, his work, as the consolidation of the United States after the death of Lincoln was still moulded by his vanished hand.

If it be true that the world's history is the world's judgment, it is no less true that the history of the state is the judgment of the statesman. Cavour would not have asked to be tried by any other criterion. He achieved a great result. He doubted if ideals of perfection could be reached, or whether, if reached, they would not be found, like mountain tops, to afford no abiding place for the foot of man. Perhaps he forgot too much that from the ice and snow of the mountain comes the river which fertilises the land. But, if he deprecated the pursuit of what he deemed the impossible, he condemned as criminal the neglect of the attainable. The charge of cynicism was unjust; Cavour was at heart an optimist; he never doubted that life was immensely worth living, that the fields open to human energy were splendid and beneficent. He hated shams, and he hated all forms of caste-feeling. He was one of the few continental statesmen who never exaggerated the power for good of government; he looked upon the private citizen who plods at his business, gives his children a good éducation, and has a reserve of savings in the funds, as the mainstay of the state.

No life of Cavour has been written since the publication of his correspondence, and of a mass of documents which throw light on his career. It has seemed more useful, therefore, within the prescribed limits, to endeavour to show what he did, and how he did it, than to give much space to the larger considerations which the Italian movement suggests. Of the ultimate issue of the events with which he was concerned it is too soon to speak. These events stand in close relation to the struggle between the civil and ecclesiastical powers, which dates back to the first assumption of political prerogatives by the Bishops of Rome. Cavour did not suffer his sovereign to eat humble pie like King John, or to go to Canossa like Henry IV., but neither did he ever entertain the wish to turn persecutor as Pombal was, perhaps, forced to do, or to browbeat the head of the Church as the first Napoleon took a pleasure in doing. He aimed at keeping the two powers separate, but each supreme in its own province.

> Content you with monopolising heaven,
> And let this little hanging ball alone ;
> For, give ye but a foot of conscience there,
> And you, like Archimedes, toss the globe.

The Italian revolution was bound up, also, with the principle of nationalities, which is still at work in South-Eastern Europe, and with the tendency towards unity which led to the refounding of the German Empire. Students who care for historical parallels will always seek to draw a comparison between Cavour and the great man who guided the new destinies of Germany. The points of resemblance are striking, but they are soon exhausted. Each undertook to free his country from extraneous influence, and to give it the strength which can only spring from union, and each was confident in his own power to succeed; either Cavour or Bismarck might have said with the younger Pitt : " I know that I can save the country, and I know no other man can." The points of disparity are inexhaustible. Prince Bismarck never threw off the aristocratico-military leanings with which he began life. He aimed at creating a strong military empire, in which the first and last duty of parliament was to vote supplies. Though the revolutionary tide set in towards unity still more in Germany than in Italy, he preferred to wait till he could do without a popular movement as an auxiliary. He did not admire the mysticism of King Frederick William IV., but he fully approved when that monarch, "the son of twenty-four electors and kings," declared that he would never accept the "iron collar" offered him by revolution "of an Imperial crown unblessed by God." Bismarck started with the immeasurable advantage that his side was the strongest. Cavour had to solve the problem of how a state of five millions could outwit an empire of thirty-seven millions. All along, the German population of Prussia was far more numerous than that of Austria, and she had allies that cost her nothing. Napoleon, as Cavour pointed out, fought for Prussia in Lombardy as much as for Piedmont. If Bismarck foresaw unification with more certainty than Cavour foresaw unity, it must be remembered that, while Cavour was held back by doubts as to whether the whole country desired unity, such doubts caused no trouble to Bismarck, since he was ready to adopt a short way with dissidents.

When Prince Bismarck once said that he was more Prussian than German, he revealed the weak side of his stupendous achievement. Prussia has not become Germany. The empire is a great defensive league in which only one participant is entirely satisfied with his position. In Italy a kingdom has grown up in which Piedmont, even to the extent of ingratitude, is forgotten. If moral fusion is still incomplete, political fusion has, at least, advanced so far that the present institutions and the nation must stand or fall together. The monarchy was made for the country, not the country for the monarchy. An acute Frenchman remarked during the Franco-German War, that Prince Bismarck had taken Cavour's conception without what made it really great—liberty. Possibly that word may still prove of better omen to the rebirth of a nation than "Blood and Iron."

CHIEF AUTHORITIES

Artom I. and A. Blanc. *Il Conte di Cavour in Parlamento.* Florence, 1868.

Bersezio, V. *Il regno di Vittorio Emanuele II.; Trent' anni di vita italiana.* Turin, 1878-95. 8 vols.

Bert, A. *Nouvelles lettres inédites de Cavour.* Turin, 1889.

Berti, D. *Il Conte di Cavour avanti al 1848.* Rome, 1886.

Bianchi, N. *La politique du Comte Camille de Cavour.* Turin, 1885.

Bonghi, R. *Ritratti contemporanei : Cavour, Bismarck, Thiers.* Milan, 1879.

Buzziconi, G. *Bibliografia Cavouriana.* Turin, 1898.

Cavour, C. *Opere politico-economiche del Conte Camillo di Cavour.* Cuneo, 1855.

—— *Discorsi parlamentari del Conte Camillo di Cavour.* Published by order of the Chamber of Deputies. Turin, 1863-72. 8 vols.

Chiala, L. *Il Conte di Cavour.* Ricordi di Michelangelo Castelli, editi per cura di L. Chiala. Turin, 1886.

—— *Lettere edite ed inedite di Camillo Cavour.* Turin, 1883-87. 7 vols.

Dicey, E. *Memoir of Cavour.* London, 1861.

La Rive (De), W. *Le Comte de Cavour. Récits et souvenirs.* Paris, 1862.

La Varenne (De), C. *Lettres inédites du Comte de Cavour au Commandeur Urbain Rattazzi.* Paris, 1862.

Mariotti, F. *La sapienza politica del Conte di Cavour e del Principe di Bismarck.* Turin, 1886.

Marriott, F. *The Makers of Modern Italy.* London, 1889.

Massari, G. *Il Conte di Cavour.* Turin, 1873.

Mazade (De), C. *Le Comte de Cavour.* Paris, 1877.

Nigra, C. *Le Comte de Cavour et la Comtesse de Circourt.* Turin, 1894.

Reumont (Von.), A. *Charakterbilder aus der neuern Geschichte Italiens.* Leipzig, 1886.

Reyntiens, M. N. *Bismarck et Cavour.* Bruxelles, 1875.

Tivaroni, C. *Storia critica del risorgimento d' Italia.* Turin, 1888-97. 9 vols.

Treitschke (Von), H. "Cavour," in *Historische und politische Aufsätze.* Leipzig, 1871.

Zanichelli, D. *Gli scritti del Conte di Cavour.* Bologna, 1892.

Also the Memoirs and Correspondence of Ricasoli, La Farina, Kossuth, Minghetti, D' Azeglio, Lanza, Arese, Della Rocca.

THE END

Printed in Great Britain by R. & R. CLARK, LIMITED, *Edinburgh.*

Foreign Statesmen Series.

Edited by J. B. BURY, M.A., Regius Professor of
Modern History at Cambridge.

Crown 8vo. 3s. 6d. net each.

CHARLES THE GREAT. By THOMAS HODGKIN,
D.C.L.

PHILIP AUGUSTUS. By the Very Rev. W. H.
HUTTON.

WILLIAM THE SILENT. By FREDERIC
HARRISON.

PHILIP THE SECOND OF SPAIN. By
Major MARTIN HUME.

RICHELIEU. By Sir R. LODGE.

MARIA THERESA. By J. FRANCK BRIGHT, D.D.

JOSEPH II. By J FRANCK BRIGHT, D.D.

MIRABEAU. By P. F. WILLERT.

COSIMO DE MEDICI. By Miss K. D. EWART.

CAVOUR. By the Countess MARTINENGO CESARESCO

MAZARIN. By ARTHUR HASSALL, M.A.

MACMILLAN AND CO., LTD., LONDON.

Twelve English Statesmen.

Edited by Viscount MORLEY.

Crown 8vo. 3s. 6d. net each.

WILLIAM THE CONQUEROR. By EDWARD A. FREEMAN, D.C.L. LL.D.

TIMES.—"Gives with great picturesqueness . . . the dramatic incidents of a memorable career far removed from our times and our manner of thinking."

HENRY II. By Mrs. J. R. GREEN.

TIMES.—"It is delightfully real and readable, and in spite of severe compression has the charm of a mediæval romance."

EDWARD I. By Prof. T. F. TOUT, M.A.

SPEAKER.—"A truer or more life-like picture of the king, the conqueror, the overlord, the duke, has never yet been drawn."

HENRY VII. By Dr. JAMES GAIRDNER.

ATHENÆUM.—"The best account of Henry VII. that has yet appeared."

CARDINAL WOLSEY. By Bishop CREIGHTON, D.D.

SATURDAY REVIEW.—"Is exactly what one of a series of short biographies of English Statesmen ought to be."

ELIZABETH. By E. S. BEESLEY, M.A.

MANCHESTER GUARDIAN.—"It may be recommended as the best and briefest and most trustworthy of the many books that in this generation have dealt with the life and deeds of that 'bright Occidental Star, Queen Elizabeth of happy memory.'"

OLIVER CROMWELL. By FREDERIC HARRISON.

TIMES.—"Gives a wonderfully vivid picture of events."

WILLIAM III. By H. D. TRAILL.

SPECTATOR.—"Mr. Traill has done his work well in the limited space at his command. The narrative portion is clear and vivacious, and his criticisms, although sometimes trenchant, are substantially just."

WALPOLE. By Viscount MORLEY.

ST. JAMES'S GAZETTE.—"It deserves to be read, not only as the work of one of the most prominent politicians of the day, but for its intrinsic merits. It is a clever, thoughtful, and interesting biography."

PITT. By Lord ROSEBERY.

TIMES.—"Brilliant and fascinating. . . . The style is terse, masculine, nervous, articulate, and clear; the grasp of circumstance and character is firm, penetrating, luminous, and unprejudiced; the judgment is broad, generous, humane, and scrupulously candid. . . . It is not only a luminous estimate of Pitt's character and policy; it is also a brilliant gallery of portraits. The portrait of Fox, for example, is a masterpiece."

PEEL. By Sir J. R. THURSFIELD, M.A.

DAILY NEWS.—"A model of what such a book should be. We can give it no higher praise than to say that it is worthy to rank with Mr. John Morley's *Walpole* in the same series."

CHATHAM. By FREDERIC HARRISON,

ST. JAMES'S GAZETTE.—"It comes near the model of what such a book should be."

MACMILLAN AND CO., LTD., LONDON.